Ireland's Field Day

Ireland's Field Day

Field Day Theatre Company

HUTCHINSON

London Melbourne Sydney Auckland Johannesburg

Hutchinson & Co. (Publishers) Ltd

An imprint of the Hutchinson Publishing Group

17-21 Conway Street, London W1P 6JD

Hutchinson Publishing Group (Australia) Pty Ltd
16-22 Church Street, Hawthorn, Melbourne, Victoria 3122

Hutchinson Group (NZ) Ltd
32-34 View Road, PO Box 40-086, Glenfield, Auckland 10

Hutchinson Group (SA) (Pty) Ltd
PO Box 337, Bergvlei 2012, South Africa

First published in pamphlet form
by Field Day Theatre Company Limited, 1983 and 1984

This edition first published 1985
© Field Day Theatre Company Limited

Set in 10pt Baskerville

Printed and bound in Great Britain by
Anchor Brendon Ltd, Tiptree, Essex

British Library Cataloguing in Publication Data

Ireland's field day.
 1. English literature—Irish authors—History and criticism   2. Politics and literature—Ireland
 I. Deane, Seamus   II. Field Day Theatre Company
 820.9'9415   PR8718

ISBN 0 09 162640 4 cased
0 09 162641 2 paper

CONTENTS

PREFACE

The Field Day Theatre Company was founded in 1980 by Brian Friel and Stephen Rea. Its birthplace and centre of operations was and continues to be the city of Derry in Northern Ireland. Since the company's opening production of Brian Friel's *Translations* in September 1980, an annual theatrical production, launched in Derry and touring thereafter throughout the whole island, has remained a central feature of the project. Stephen Rea has played a leading role in all the plays and has directed some. After *Translations*, there were Brian Friel's adaptation of Chekhov's *Three Sisters* (1981), his *The Communication Cord* (1982), Athol Fugard's *Boesman and Lena* (1983) and, in 1984, a double bill including Tom Paulin's version of *Antigone* entitled *The Riot Act* and Derek Mahon's verse translation of Molière's *Ecole des Maris* entitled *High Time*. All these productions were financed by the Arts Councils of Northern Ireland and of the Republic of Ireland.

Before *Translations* inaugurated the company's public activities, the initial project for a new theatre and a new audience had been widened. Four others were invited to join the company as directors — Seamus Heaney, Tom Paulin, David Hammond and Seamus Deane. In brief, all the directors felt that the political crisis in the North and its reverberations in the Republic had made the necessity of a reappraisal of Ireland's political and cultural situation explicit and urgent. All of the directors are northerners. They believed that Field Day could and should contribute to the solution of the present crisis by producing analyses of the established opinions, myths and stereotypes which had become both a symptom and a cause of the current situation. The collapse of constitutional and political arrangements and the recrudescence of the violence which they had been designed to repress or contain, made this a more urgent requirement in the North than in the Republic, even though the improbability of either surviving in its present form seemed clear in 1980 and is clearer still in 1985.

The company decided, therefore, to embark upon a succession of publications, starting with a series of pamphlets, in which the nature of the Irish problem could be explored and, as a result, more successfully confronted that it had been hitherto. The pamphlets were published in groups of three, in September 1983 and May 1984. A third series is appearing in the Autumn of 1985. Three Field Day directors — Heaney, Paulin and Deane — wrote the first series; two others, not members of Field Day, Declan Kiberd and Richard Kearney, joined with Deane in the second series. The third series, on the Protestant Idea of Liberty, has no Field Day director among the authors. In addition, Field Day published Seamus Heaney's *Sweeney Astray* in November 1983.

It is intended that a variety of publications will appear in the next few years, all of them designed to introduce or reintroduce new or relatively ignored material — essays, poems, fiction — which the company believes will enrich or illuminate awareness of the complex nature of the Irish tradition in writing. A central ambition in this regard will be the production of a large-scale anthology of Irish writing in the last 500 years. This anthology will have the aim of revealing and confirming the existence of a continuous tradition, contributed to by all groups, sects and parties, in which the possibility of a more generous and hospitable notion of Ireland's cultural achievements will emerge as the basis for a more ecumenical and eirenic approach to the deep and apparently implacable problems which confront the island today.

Field Day Theatre Company
Derry
March 1985

A New Look at the Language Question

by Tom Paulin

Tom Paulin   Born in Leeds and grew up in Belfast. Lecturer in English at Nottingham University since 1972. Visiting Associate Professor of English and Fulbright Scholar at the University of Virginia 1983-4.

Publications include: poetry — *A State of Justice* (1977), *The Strange Museum* (1980), *Liberty Tree* (1983); criticism — *Thomas Hardy: The Poetry of Perception* (1977), *Ireland and the English Crisis* (1984).

His version of the *Antigone* of Sophocles entitled *The Riot Act* was produced by Field Day in 1984 and recently published by Faber and Faber.

Winner of the Eric Gregory Award, the Somerset Maugham Award and the Geoffrey Faber Award. A Director of Field Day.

1

A NEW LOOK AT
THE LANGUAGE QUESTION

The history of a language is often a story of possession and
dispossession, territorial struggle and the establishment or
imposition of a culture. Arguments about the 'evolution' or the
'purity' of a language can be based on a simplistic notion of
progress or on a doctrine of racial stereotypes. Thus a
Spenserian phrase which Samuel Johnson employs in the
famous preface to his dictionary — 'the wells of English
undefiled' — is instinct with a mystic and exclusive idea of
nationhood. It defines a language and a culture in terms of a
chimerical idea of racial purity. But Johnson doesn't profess
this idea either visibly or aggressively, and in the less well-
known essay which follows his preface he comments on the
historical sources of the English language. Reflecting on the
extinction of the ancient British language, he remarks:

> it is scarcely possible that a nation, however depressed,
> should have been mixed in considerable numbers with the
> Saxons without some communication of their tongue, and
> therefore it may, with great reason, be imagined, that
> those, who were not sheltered in the mountains, perished
> by the sword.

Anglo-Saxon society was among the very first European
societies to establish a tradition of vernacular prose. However,
for several centuries after the Norman conquest English was
regarded as a rude and uncultivated tongue. At the beginning
of the fourteenth century, the chronicler Robert of Gloucester
notes with concern that English is spoken only by 'lowe men'.
He remarks that England is the only country in the world which
doesn't 'hold' to its own speech, and implies that such a
situation is unnatural. Here he is clearly influenced by the
English nationalism which developed after the crown lost
Normandy early in the thirteenth century. French, however,
continued to be the official language of England until a
parliamentary statute of 1362 stated that all law suits must be
conducted in English. French was displaced and English
returned from a form of internal exile.

The English language was first brought to Ireland by the followers of Strongbow's Norman invaders in the twelfth century. Norman French and English became established as vernacular languages, though their speakers gradually crossed over to Irish. Attempts were made to resist this process — for example in the statutes of Kilkenny (1366) — but the irishing of the settlers was completed by the Reformation which united the 'Old English' with the native Irish against the protestant 'New English'. And as Alan Bliss has shown, the Cromwellian Settlement of the 1650s was to be crucial to the history of the English language in Ireland. With the exception of Ulster, the English spoken in most parts of Ireland today is descended from the language of Cromwell's planters. The result, according to Diarmaid Ó Muirithe, is 'a distinctive Irish speech — Anglo-Irish or Hiberno-English, call it what you will'.

In England, the English language reached a peak of creative power during the Elizabethan and Jacobean periods when writers formed sentences by instinct or guesswork rather than by stated rule. In time it was felt that the language was overseeded and in need of more careful cultivation. Writers began to argue that the absence of a standard of 'correct' English created an ugly and uncivilized linguistic climate, and Dryden remarked that he sometimes had to translate an idea into Latin before he could decide on the proper way of expressing it in English. In a *Discourse Concerning Satire* he noted, 'we have yet no prosodia, not so much as a tolerable dictionary, or a grammar, so that our language is in a manner barbarous'. Dryden's neoclassicism had an epic scope and power and like Virgil's Aeneas he wished to found a new *civitas* in a country damaged by violence and conflict. He argued that in order to properly regulate and refine the language England must have an academy modelled on the Académie Française. His criticism of the state of the language was developed by Swift in *A Proposal for Correcting, Improving, and Ascertaining the English Tongue,* which was addressed to Robert Harley, the Lord High Treasurer of England, and published in 1712. Although Swift strategically avoided mentioning the idea of an academy, it is clear that he intended his readers to make that deduction. Only an academy would be capable of 'ascertaining and fixing our language for ever, after such alterations are made in it as shall be thought requisite'.

Swift's proposal appears to be innocent of political interest, but a Whig paper, the *Medley,* detected Jacobitism in his preference for the romance languages over the Saxon on the grounds that he was opposed to any 'new addition of Saxon words by bringing over the Hanover family'. According to his

Whig critic, Swift wished to hasten 'a new invasion by the Pretender and the French, because that language has more Latin words than the Saxon'. Partly as a result, the idea of an academy came to be regarded as essentially unpatriotic, and it was on these grounds that Johnson took issue with Swift's 'petty treatise'. In the preface to his dictionary he remarks that he does not wish 'to see dependence multiplied' and hopes that 'the spirit of English liberty' will hinder or destroy any attempt to set up an academy in England. Although Matthew Arnold revived Swift's proposal in a provocative essay entitled 'The Literary Influence of Academies', the idea of an academic legislature for the language was effectively extinguished by Johnson's preface.

Johnson's argument is insular, aggressive and somewhat sentimental, yet there can be no doubt that he is expressing an ingrained cultural hostility to state intervention in the language. Johnson believed that a dictionary could perform the function of correcting English better than an academy could, and he argued that the organic nature of language ought to be respected. It was both misguided and tyrannical to attempt to freeze the English language artificially as Swift had suggested.

Johnson's English patriotism and his anarchistic conservatism inform his view of the language, and in accordance with his libertarian principles he avoids imposing any guide to pronunciation in his dictionary. Swift, however, advocated a standard English pronunciation and in an essay 'On Barbarous Denominations in Ireland' he criticised the Scottish accent and most English regional accents as 'offensive'. He also observed that an Irish accent made 'the deliverer . . . ridiculous and despised', and remarked that 'from such a mouth, an Englishman expects nothing but bulls, blunders, and follies'. For Swift, a standard English accent is a platonic ideal which will give dignity and self-respect to anyone who acquires it. He is therefore rejecting a concept of 'Hiberno-English' or 'Anglo-Irish' and is advocating a unified culture which embraces both Britain and Ireland. This ideal of complete integration still has its supporters, but it must now be apparent that a Unionist who retains a marked Irish accent is either an unconscious contradiction or a subversive ironist.

Dictionaries generally do legislate for pronunciation and towards the end of the eighteenth century a 'war of the dictionaries' took place in England. The argument was between supporters of Thomas Sheridan's 'pronouncing dictionary' and those who preferred John Walker's rival dictionary. Sheridan had what Johnson termed 'the disadvantage of being an Irishman' and so was not allowed to fix the pronunciation of

English. On patriotic grounds the controversy was therefore decided in Walker's favour.

If sentiments about the English language can at times be informed by an idea of ethnicity, attempts to refine and ascertain the language almost instinctively relate it to the houses of parliament, to those institutions where speech exercises power. In his *Dictionary of Modern English Usage* H. W. Fowler frequently draws examples from parliamentary debates, and in this entry he reveals the simple patriotism which fires his concept of correct usage:

> *England, English(man).* The incorrect use of these words as equivalents of *Great Britain* or *The United Kingdom, British, Briton,* is often resented by other nationals of the U.K., like the book-reviewer who writes of Lord Cherwell's 'dedication to the service of Britain, which, in the annoying way foreigners have, he persisted in calling "England"'. Their susceptibilities are natural, but are not necessarily always to be deferred to. For many purposes the wider words are the natural ones. We speak of the *British Commonwealth,* the *British Navy, Army,* and *Air Force* and *British trade;* we boast that *Britons* never never shall be slaves; we know that Sir John Moore sleeps in a grave where a *Briton* has laid him, and there is no alternative to *British* English if we want to distinguish our idiom from the American. But it must be remembered that no Englishman, or perhaps no Scotsman even, calls himself a Briton without a sneaking sense of the ludicrous, or hears himself referred to as a BRITISHER without squirming. How should an Englishman utter·the words *Great Britain* with the glow of emotion that for him goes with *England?* His sovereign may be Her *Brittanic* Majesty to outsiders, but to him is Queen of *England;* he talks the *English* language; he has been taught *English* history as one continuous tale from Alfred to his own day; he has heard of the word of an *Englishman* and aspires to be an *English* gentleman; and he knows that *England* expects every man to do his duty. 'Speak for *England'* was the challenge flung across the floor of the House of Commons by Leo Amery to the leader of the Opposition on 2 Sept. 1939. In the word *England,* not in *Britain* all these things are implicit. It is unreasonable to ask forty millions of people to refrain from the use of the only names that are in tune with patriotic emotion or to make them stop and think whether they mean their country in a narrower or wider sense each time they name it.

More recently, a Conservative member of parliament praised Michael Foot for 'speaking for England' during the comic and hysterical debate which followed Argentina's invasion of the Malvinas Islands. It would appear that at moments of crisis in the United Kingdom a ruling Englishness overcomes the less satisfying concept, British.

Englishness is an instinctual, ethnic identification, while the relatively recent concept, British, lacks its inspirational power. Indeed, as Fowler demonstrates, some English people feel a form of cultural cringe in relation to the imperial label, and in the 1980s terms like 'British car', 'British justice' or 'British industry' have increasingly either a less confident or a downright pejorative usage within England. In many ways, this new usage is connected with a movement of consciousness which Tom Nairn has termed 'the break-up of Britain'. On the other hand, Great Britain is a society composed of many different ethnic cultures and those who identify with it would argue that the term 'British' can be seen as inclusive, positive and multi-racial, where 'English' may be construed in an exclusive and negative manner. Again, many West Indians and Asians would reject this idea and argue that racist attitudes are on the increase in Britain.

Fundamentally, the language question is a question about nationhood and government, and some lexicographers perceive an occult connection between the English language and the English constitution. Johnson appears to have initiated the analogy when he concluded his attack on the idea of an academy by saying, 'we have long preserved our constitution, let us make some struggles for our language'. James Murray, the editor-in-chief of the *New English Dictionary*, developed this analogy when he observed that 'the English Dictionary, like the English Constitution, is the creation of no one man, and of no one age; it is a growth that has slowly developed itself down the ages'. Murray also compared Johnson's work to a 'lexicographic cairn' and so added a sense of primitive magic to the idea of anonymous tradition which he was asserting. Murray's twin comparisons to cairn and constitution help to infuse a magisterial, legislative authority with a form of natural piety that is partly the expression of his Scottishness. For Swift's platonic or rational ideal of complete integration and classic standardization, Murray substitutes a slightly lichened idea of the dictionary as the equivalent of Wordsworth's leechgatherer. It is both book and sacred natural object, one of the guardians of the nation's soul. And because the *New English Dictionary* was dedicated to Queen Victoria the imaginative power of the crown was joined to the natural magic of the cairn and the reverential power of the unwritten constitution. Thus the *NED*, or *Oxford English Dictionary* as it became, stands as one of the cornerstones of the culture which created it. It is a monumental work of scholarship and possesses a quasi-divine authority.

The *Oxford English Dictionary* is the chief lexicon of a language which can be more accurately described as 'British English'. In a sense, its compilers worked in the shadow of Noah Webster's *An American Dictionary of the English Language.*[1] Something of the rivalry which Murray's team felt with American culture is reflected in the single example of a 'typical' reader's quotation-slip which is given in the preface to the *NED*:

> Britisher
>
> 1883 Freeman Impressions U.S. iv. 29 I always told my American friends that I had rather be called a Britisher than an Englishman, if by calling me an English-man they meant to imply that they were not Englishmen themselves.

The disinterested scholar, laboriously and often thanklessly at work on a dictionary, cannot fail to have first asked himself this fundamental question: for what nation am I compiling this lexicon? Murray's identification with Victorian Britain and his sense of the importance of the Scottish scholarly tradition to that cultural hegemony clearly inspired his labours.

The career of Noah Webster, like that of James Murray, was partly fired by an inherited Calvinism, but it was a career dedicated to overthrowing, not consolidating, an imperial hegemony. Webster had to challenge the dominating force of Johnson's dictionary and personality. And the challenge he mounted was so effective that Webster's *Dictionary of American English* became a great originating work, the scholarly equivalent of an epic poem or of a prose epic like *Ulysses*.

Webster was born in 1758 and served briefly in the American Revolution. While working as a schoolteacher he became dissatisfied with textbooks which ignored American culture. He was convinced that America needed a uniform language, its own school books and its own intellectual life. In 1783 he published his famous 'Blue-Backed Speller' or

---

1 Published in 1828. The change in title from *A Dictionary of the American Language* (1800) reflects Webster's growing conservatism.

American Spelling Book and this initiated his concept of linguistic separation. The social and political totality of that concept is expressed in an influential pamphlet of 1778 in which he advocated the adoption of the Federal Constitution. Two years later, in his *Dissertations on the English Language,* Webster offered a powerful argument for linguistic and cultural independence.

In the *Dissertations* Webster attacks Johnson's lumpy neo-classicism, criticising him for the 'intolerable' Latinity of his style and for a pedantry which has 'corrupted the purity of our language'. He argues that it is essential for America to grow away from the concept of language and nationality which Johnson's dictionary enforces:

> As an independent nation, our honor requires us to have a system of our own, in language as well as government. Great Britain, whose children we are, and whose language we speak, should no longer be *our* standard; for the taste of her writers is already corrupted, and her language on the decline.

Webster argues that 'uniformity of speech' helps to form 'national attachments', while local accents hinder a sense of national identity. Here his argument resembles Dante's in *De Vulgari Eloquentia,* for like Dante he is advocating a language that is common to every region without being tied to any particular locality.

In a concluding appeal, Webster states:

> Let us then seize the present moment, and establish a *national language,* as well as a national government. Let us remember that there is a certain respect due to the opinions of other nations. As an independent people, our reputation abroad demands that, in all things, we should be federal; be *national;* for if we do not respect *ourselves,* we may be assured that *other nations* will not respect us. In short, let it be impressed upon the mind of every American, that to neglect the means of commanding respect abroad, is treason against the character and dignity of a brave independent people.

Like Swift, whose Gulliver he echoes,[2] Webster argues for linguistic self-respect, but he does so as a separatist, not an integrationist. His classicism is national and federal, and does not aspire to a platonic norm which transcends the nationalities inhabiting different countries. This separatist idea has been

---

2 In "A Voyage to Lilliput" Gulliver protests that he 'would never be an instrument of bringing a free and brave people into slavery'.

influential and there now exist a *Scottish National Dictionary*, a *Dictionary of Canadianisms on Historical Principles*, and a *Dictionary of Jamaican English*.

Webster's dictionary and the concept of American English which it embodies succeeded in making that language appear to be a native growth. In Ireland, the English language has been traditionally regarded as an imposed colonial tongue and Irish as the autochthonous language of the island. British policy was hostile to Irish and in 1904, for example, a Commissioner of National Education wrote to Douglas Hyde, 'I will use all my influence, as in the past, to ensure that Irish as a spoken language shall die out as quickly as possible'. However, as Seán De Fréine has argued, the movement away from Irish in the 19th century was not the product of 'any law or official regulation'. Instead it was the result of a 'social self-generated movement of collective behaviour among the people themselves'. English was the language of power, commerce and social acceptance, and the Irish people largely accepted Daniel O'Connell's view that Gaelic monolingualism was an obstacle to freedom. Particularly after the Famine, parents encouraged their children to learn English as this would help them make new lives in America.

Although the conflict between English and Irish can be compared to the struggle between Anglo-Saxon and Old British, such an analogy conceals the ironies and complexities of the problem. This is because the English language in Ireland, like English in America, became so naturalised that it appeared to be indigenous. The Irish language, however, was not completely suppressed or rejected, and it became central to the new national consciousness which formed late in the 19th century. As a result of the struggle for independence it was re-instated as the national language of a country which comprised three provinces and three counties of the four ancient provinces of Ireland. It forms an important part of the school syllabus in the Irish Republic, is on the syllabus of schools administered by the Roman Catholic Church in Northern Ireland, and is absent from the curricula of Northern Irish state schools.

Traditionally, a majority of Unionist protestants have regarded the Irish language as belonging exclusively to Irish catholic culture. Although this is a misapprehension, it helps to confirm the essentially racist ethic which influences some sections of Unionist opinion and which is also present in the old-fashioned nationalist concept of the 'pure Gael'. As a result, Unionist schools are monolingual while non-Unionist schools offer some counterbalance to English monolingualism.

Put another way, state education in Northern Ireland is based upon a pragmatic view of the English language and a short-sighted assumption of colonial status, while education in the Irish Republic is based on an idealistic view of Irish which aims to conserve the language and assert the cultural difference of the country.

Although there are scholarly studies of 'Hiberno English' and 'Ulster English',[3] the language appears at the present moment to be in a state of near anarchy. Spoken Irish English exists in a number of provincial and local forms, but because no scholar has as yet compiled a *Dictionary of Irish English* many words are literally homeless. They live in the careless richness of speech, but they rarely appear in print. When they do, many readers are unable to understand them and have no dictionary where they can discover their meaning. The language therefore lives freely and spontaneously as speech, but it lacks any institutional existence and so is impoverished as a literary medium. It is a language without a lexicon, a language without form. Like some strange creature of the open air, it exists simply as *Geist* or spirit.

Here, a fundamental problem is the absence of a classic style of discursive prose. Although Yeats argues for a tradition of cold, sinewy and passionate Anglo-Irish prose, this style is almost defunct now. Where it still exists it appears both bottled and self-conscious, and no distinctive new style has replaced it. Contributors to *The Irish Times* — Owen Dudley Edwards, for example — tend to write in a slack and blathery manner, while *The Belfast Newsletter* offers only a form of rasping business-man's prose. *The Irish Press* differs from *The Irish Times* in having an exemplary literary editor, but its copy-editing is not of a high standard.[4] And although Irish historians often like to congratulate themselves on their disinterested purity, a glance at the prose of F.S.L. Lyons reveals a style drawn from the claggy fringes of local journalism.[5]

---

3   Notably by Alan Bliss and John Braidwood. Professor Braidwood is at present compiling an Ulster Dialect Dictionary. A dictionary of Hiberno-English, which was begun under the auspices of the Royal Irish Academy, has been abandoned due to lack of funds.

4   E.g. 'Born in Rathdrum, Co. Wicklow, where her father was a flour miller, she was educated privately and later at a convent school but, when her father died, when she was 14, she was told that she would have to learn to earn her own living'. Obituary of Maire Comerford in *The Irish Press* 16/12/82.

5   E.g. 'Nevertheless, the university remained the objective and as Charles settled into harness his work and even, apparently, his manners, improved and we learn of village cricket (he was that valuable commodity, a good wicket-keeper-batsman) and of frequent invitations to dances. And at last Cambridge materialized'. *Charles Stewart Parnell*, chapter one.

Perhaps the alternative to a style based on assorted Deasyisms,[6] is a form of ideal, international English? Samuel Beckett's prose is a repudiation of the provincial nature of Hiberno-English in favour of a stateless language which is an English passed through the cartesian rigours of the French language. In its purity, elegance and simplicity, Beckett's language is a version of the platonic standard which Swift recommended nearly three centuries ago in his *Proposal*. Paradoxically, though, Beckett's language is both purer than Swift's and yet inhabited by faint, wistful presences which emanate from Hiberno-English.

Most people, however, demand that the language which they speak has a much closer contact with their native or habitual climate. Here, dialect is notable for its intimacy and for the bonds which it creates among speakers. Standard speech frequently gives way to dialect when people soothe or talk to small children, and sexual love, too, is often expressed through dialect words. Such words are local and 'warm', while their standard alternatives can be regarded as coldly public and extra-familial. Often a clash is felt between the intimacy of dialect — from which a non-standard accent is inseparable — and the demands of a wider professional world where standard speech and accent are the norm. For English people such tensions are invariably a product of the class system, but in Ireland they spring from more complex loyalties (listeners to last year's Reith lectures will have noticed how Denis Donoghue's accent oscillates between educated southern speech and a slight Ulster ululation).

If Donoghue speaks for a partitioned island, G. B. Thompson speaks for a divided culture:

> As to the content of the book I must confess to being ill-equipped to comment on it. I am not a serious student of dialect, and any knowledge I have of the subject comes from the fact that as a native of County Antrim my first "language" was the Ulster-Scots dialect of the area, described elsewhere in this book by G. B. Adams and by my fellow townsman Robert Gregg. Eventually, like so many others before and since, I was 'educated' to the point where I looked upon dialect as merely a low-class, ungrammatical way of speaking. The essays in this book, therefore, have been a revelation to me, and I find myself hoping that my experience will be shared by others who have not as yet come to realize the full significance of

---

6   See Mr Deasy's letter about foot-and-mouth disease in the 'Nestor' chapter of *Ulysses*.

Ulster dialect, but who may still see it as merely a source of humour and the language of Ulster's folk plays — the kitchen comedies. That it can be, and often is, incomparably humorous is undeniable, but it also makes for eloquence of power and beauty, and if this book were to do no more than help to raise the popular conception of our dialect above the level of the after-dinner story it would serve a useful purpose.[7]

This statement was made in 1964 and with hindsight we can detect in it a slight movement of consciousness towards the separatist idea which is now held by a significant section of 'loyalist' opinion. Nearly twenty years later, Ian Adamson has offered an account of language which is wholly separatist in intention. It is a response to the homeless or displaced feeling which is now such a significant part of the loyalist imagination, and its historical teleology points to an independent Ulster where socialist politics have replaced the sectarian divisions of the past.

Adamson is in some ways the most interesting of recent loyalist historians because he writes from the dangerous and intelligent edges of that consciousness. In 'The Language of Ulster' Adamson argues that the province's indigenous language — Old British — was displaced by Irish, just as Irish was later displaced by English. In this way he denies an absolute territorial claim to either community in Northern Ireland and this allows him to argue for a concept of 'our homeland' which includes both communities. His account of an ancient British, or Cruthin, people is a significant influence on the UDA's Ulster nationalism and forms an influential part of that organization's hostility to the British state.

Where the IRA seeks to make a nation out of four provinces, the UDA aspires to make six counties of one province into an independent nation. Official Unionism, on the other hand, tries to conserve what remains of the Act of Union and clings to a concept of nationality which no longer satisfies many of the British people whom the Unionists wish to identify with. This can now be observed in England where the movement of opinion against Cruise missiles and the continuing demonstration at Greenham Common exemplify that alternative English nationalism which is expressed in Blake's vision of Albion and reflected in the writings of E.P. Thompson. Despite the recent election, this visionary commitment is still a powerful force within English society and it is connected with

7   Preface to *Ulster Dialects: An Introductory Symposium.*

the shift in public opinion in favour of withdrawal from Northern Ireland.

Adamson's historical myth necessarily involves the concept of a national language, and he is deeply conscious of the need to prove that he speaks a language which is as indigenous — or as nearly indigenous — as Irish. He argues:

> Neither Ulster Lallans nor Ulster English are 'foreign' since the original dialects were modified in the mouths of the local Gaelic speakers who acquired them and eventually, after a bilingual period, lost their native tongue. These modified dialects were then gradually adopted by the Scottish and English settlers themselves, since the Irish constituted the majority population. The dialect of Belfast is a variety of Ulster English, so that the people of the Shankill Road speak English which is almost a literal translation of Gaelic.

Adamson's argument is obviously vulnerable and yet it forms part of a worthwhile attempt to offer a historical vision which goes beyond traditional barriers. The inclusive and egalitarian nature of his vision also ensures that it lacks the viciousness of the historical myth which was purveyed by the notorious Tara organization, blessed by the Reverend Martin Smyth and other leading Unionists, and which figured so prominently in the still unresolved Kincora scandal.[8]

In *The Identity of Ulster* Adamson reveals that the loyalist community he speaks for is conscious of itself as a 'minority people'. Like the Irish language, Lallans — or Ulster Scots — is

---

8 'On 28th June 1970 Ireland's Heritage Orange Lodge was founded. This was largely a reflection of McGrath's ideas although the Lodge had originally been associated with St Mary's Church of Ireland on Belfast's Crumlin Road and many members shared an obscure sense of Irish identity. It seems to me that many Ulster protestants have an identity crisis. They don't really like to think of themselves as British, and the Irish Republic has become a foreign nation, with strange ways, to most protestants. The Lodge did however seem to awaken in many a sense of Irishness which was not uncomfortable. It seems that the objective in having an "Irish" Orange Lodge was to provide a legitimate means of promoting McGrath's ideas. Rev. Martin Smyth and Rev. John Bryans, who was also known as a British Israelite though a non-militant one and was Grand Master of the Orange Order at the time, took part in the inauguration of the Lodge. We sang a hymn from McGrath's hymn book, "Let me carry your cross for Ireland Lord" which had been written by Thomas Ashe, an IRA hunger-striker who died in a Dublin jail in 1917. Dr Hillery, the Irish Minister for External Affairs at the time, corresponded with the Lodge soon after it was founded and two Irish Government Bulletins were produced depicting the Lodge Banner and carrying the correspondence. McGrath earlier proposed that the flags of the four Irish provinces be carried but rejected any suggestion that the six county Ulster flag be carried'.
Roy Garland in *The Irish Times* 15/4/82.

threatened by the English language and Adamson calls for the preservation of both languages within an Independent Ulster. However, a hostile critic would argue that Adamson's work springs from the same idea of 'ould dacency' which renders Benedict Kiely's fictions so evasively sentimental. Although the leaders of the main political parties in the Irish Republic have paid at least lip service to the idea of a 'pluralist' state with safeguards for minorities, it is clear that most loyalists distrust them almost as much as they distrust British politicians. Adamson therefore offers an alternative to both the Irish Republic and the United Kingdom. But one of the weaknesses in his argument is an uncertainty about the status and the nature of the English language in Ireland. He sees Ulster Scots as oppressed by educated 'Ulster English' — the provincial language of Official Unionism, for example — but he lacks a concept of Irish English. This is because Adamson, like G. B. Thompson, is unwilling to contemplate the all-Ireland context which a federal concept of Irish English would necessarily express. Such a concept would redeem many words from that too-exclusive, too-local, usage which amounts to a kind of introverted neglect. Many words which now appear simply gnarled, or which 'make strange' or seem opaque to most readers, would be released into the shaped flow of a new public language. Thus in Ireland there would exist three fully-fledged languages — Irish, Ulster Scots and Irish English. Irish and Ulster Scots would be preserved and nourished, while Irish English would be a form of modern English which draws on Irish, the Yola and Fingallian dialects, Ulster Scots, Elizabethan English, Hiberno-English, British English and American English. A confident concept of Irish English would substantially increase the vocabulary and this would invigorate the written language. A language that lives lithely on the tongue ought to be capable of becoming the flexible written instrument of a complete cultural idea.

Until recently, few Irish writers appear to have felt frustrated by the absence of a dictionary which might define those words which are in common usage in Ireland, but which do not appear in the *OED*. This is possibly because most writers have instinctively moulded their language to the expectations of the larger audience outside Ireland. The result is a language which lives a type of romantic, unfettered existence — no dictionary accommodates it, no academy regulates it, no common legislative body speaks it, and no national newspaper guards it. Thus the writer who professes this language must either explain dialect words tediously in a glossary or restrict his audience at each particular 'dialectical' moment. A writer who employs a word like 'geg' or 'gulder' or Kavanagh's lovely 'gobshite', will create a form of closed, secret communication with readers who come from the same region. This will express something very near to a familial relationship because every family has its hoard of relished words which express its members' sense of kinship. These words act as a kind of secret sign and serve to exclude the outside world. They constitute a dialect of endearment within the wider dialect.

In the case of some northern Irish writers — John Morrow, for example — dialect words can be over-used, while southern Irish writers sometimes appear to have been infected by Frank Delaney's saccharine gabbiness. However, the Irish writer who excludes dialect words altogether runs the risk of wilfully impoverishing a rich linguistic resource. Although there might be, somewhere, a platonic Unionist author who believes that good prose should always be as close as possible to Standard British English, such an aspiration must always be impossible for any Irish writer. This is because the platonic standard has an actual location — it isn't simply free and transcendental — and that location is the British House of Commons. There, in moments of profound crisis, people speak exclusively 'for England'. On such occasions, all dialect words are the subject of an invisible exclusion-order and archaic Anglo-Norman words like 'treason' and 'vouch' are suddenly dunted into a kind of life.

There may exist, however, a type of modern English which offers an alternative to Webster's patriotic argument (Imagist poetry, for example, is written in a form of minimal international English). Beckett's language is obviously a form of this cosmopolitan English and some Irish writers would argue that this is the best available language. By such an argument, it is perfectly possible to draw on, say, French and Irish without being aligned with a particular concept of society. For creative writers this can adumbrate a pure civility which should not be pressed into the service of history or politics.

This is not the case with discursive writers who must start from a concept of civil duty and a definite cultural affiliation. Discursive prose is always committed in some sense or other and it is dishonest to pretend that it isn't. Historiography and literary criticism are related to journalism, however much historians of the new brahmin school resist such an 'impure' relation. Indeed, a language can live both gracefully and intensely in its literary and political journalism. Unfortunately, the establishment of a tradition of good critical prose, like the publication of *A Dictionary of Irish English* or the rewriting of the Irish Constitution, appear to be impossible in the present climate of confused opinions and violent politics. One of the results of this enormous cultural impoverishment is a living, but fragmented speech, untold numbers of homeless words, and an uncertain or a derelict prose.

BIBLIOGRAPHY

G. B. Adams, ed,	*Ulster Dialects: An Introductory Symposium* (1964)
Ian Adamson	'The Language of Ulster' in *The Identity of Ulster* (1982)
A. C. Baugh	*A History of the English Language* (1965)
Alan Bliss	*Spoken English in Ireland: 1600-1740* (1979)
John Braidwood	'Ulster and Elizabethan English' in *Ulster Dialects* *The Ulster Dialect Lexicon* (1969)
H. W. Fowler	*A Dictionary of Modern English Usage* (1965)
James Root Hulbert	*Dictionaries British and American* (1955)
Samuel Johnson	Preface to *A Dictionary of the English Language* (1755) 'The History of the English Language' in *A Dictionary of the English Language*
H. L. Mencken	*The American Language* (1937)
James Milroy	*Regional Accents of English: Belfast* (1981)
James A. H. Murray	*The Evolution of English Lexicography* (1900)
K. M. Elisabeth Murray	*Caught in the Web of Words: James Murray and the Oxford English Dictionary* (1977)
Diarmaid Ó Muirithe, ed,	*The English Language in Ireland* (1977)
John Pepper	*What a Thing to Say* (1977)
Jonathan Swift	*A Proposal for Correcting, Improving, and Ascertaining the English Tongue* (1712)
G. B. Thompson	Preface to *Ulster Dialects*
Noah Webster	*The American Spelling Book* (1783) *Dissertations on the English Language* (1789)

An Open Letter

by Seamus Heaney

Seamus Heaney   Publications include *Death of A Naturalist* (1966), *Door Into the Dark* (1969), *Wintering Out* (1972), *North* (1975), *Field Work* (1979), *Preoccupations: Selected Prose 1968-78* (1980), *Sweeney Astray* (1983) and *Station Island* (1984).

Winner of Somerset Maugham Award, Cholmondeley Award, Irish Academy Foundation Award, and many others.

A graduate of Queen's University, Belfast, from which he has received an Honorary Doctorate, he is now Boylston Professor at Harvard University. A Director of Field Day.

What is the source of our first suffering?
It lies in the fact that we hesitated to speak . . .
It was born in the moment when we accumulated
silent things within us.

GASTON BACHELARD

2

AN OPEN LETTER

1   To Blake and Andrew, Editors,
Contemporary British Verse,
Penguin Books, Middlesex. Dear Sirs,
     My anxious muse,
Roused on her bed among the furze,
     Has to refuse

2   The adjective. It makes her blush.
It brings her out in a hot flush.
Before this she was called "British"
     And acquiesced
But this time it's like the third wish,
     The crucial test.

3   Caesar's Britain, its *partes tres,*
United England, Scotland, Wales,
Britannia in the old tales,
     Is common ground.
Hibernia is where the Gaels
     Made a last stand

4   And long ago were stood upon—
End of simple history lesson.
As empire rings its curtain down
     This "British" word
Sticks deep in native and *colon*
     Like Arthur's sword.

5   For weeks and months I've messed about,
Unclear, embarrassed and in doubt,
Footered, havered, spraughled, wrought
      Like Shauneen Keogh,
Wondering should I write it out
      Or let it go.

6   Anything for a quiet life.
Play possum and pretend you're deaf.
When awkward facts nag like the wife
      Look blank, go dumb.
To greet the smiler with the knife
      Smile back at him.

7   And what price then, self-preservation?
Your silence is an abdication.
Your Prince of Denmark hesitation
      You'll expiate
In Act Five, in desperation —
      Too much, too late.

8   And therefore it is time to break
Old inclinations not to speak
Which you defined already, Blake,
      Good advocate,
But if I clammed now for your sake
      I'd always rue it.

9   To think the title *Opened Ground*
Was the first title in your mind!
To think of where the phrase was found
      Makes it far worse!
To be supplanted in the end
      By *British* verse.

10   "Under a common flag," said Larkin.
      "Different history," said Haughton.
      Our own fastidious John Jordan
          Raised an eyebrow:
      How British were the Ulstermen?
          He'd like to know.

11   Answer: as far as we are part
      Of a new commonwealth of art,
      Salute with independent heart
          And equally
      Doff and flourish in your court
          Of poesie.

12   (I'll stick to *I*. Forget the *we*.
      As Livy said, *pro se quisque*.
      And Horace was exemplary
          At Philippi:
      He threw away his shield to be
          A naked *I*.)

13   Yet doubts, admittedly, arise
      When somebody who publishes
      In LRB and TLS,
          The Listener—
      In other words, whose audience is,
          Via Faber,

14   A British one, is characterized
      As British. But don't be surprised
      If I demur, for, be advised
          My passport's green.
      No glass of ours was ever raised
          To toast *The Queen*.

15   No harm to her nor you who deign
     To *God Bless* her as sovereign,
     Except that from the start her reign
               Of crown and rose
     Defied, displaced, would not combine
               What I'd espouse.

16   You'll understand I draw the line
     At being robbed of what is mine,
     My *patria,* my deep design
               To be at home
     In my own place and dwell within
               Its proper name—

17   Traumatic Ireland! Checkpoints, cairns,
     Slated roofs, stone ditches, ferns,
     Dublin squares where sunset burns
               The Georgian brick—
     The whole imagined country mourns
               Its lost, erotic

18   *Aisling* life. But I digress.
     "The pang of ravishment." Now guess
     The author of that sweet hurt phrase.
               Lawrence? Wilde?
     No way, my friends. In fact it was
               That self-exiled,

19   Vigilant, anti-cavalier,
     Anti-pornographic, fear-
     some scourge of diction that's impure,
               That Royal Navy
     Poet of water-nymph and shire:
               Donald Davie.

20   The pattern of the patriot
        Is Davie's theme: all polyglot
        Newspeak conference flies he'd swot
                Who *lhude sing*
        Foucault, Foucault. But that is not,
                Just now, my thing.

21   It is the way his words imply
        That *patria* is maidenly
        (Is "pang of ravishment" not O.K.?)
                That touched me most
        Who long felt my identity
                So rudely forc'd.

22   Tereu. Tereu. And tooraloo.
        A shudder in the loins. And so
        The twins for Leda. And twins too
                For the hurt North,
        One island-green, one royal blue.
                An induced birth.

23   One a Provo, one a Para,
        One Law and Order, one Terror—
        It's time to break the cracked mirror
                Of this conceit.
        It leads nowhere so why bother
                To work it out?

24   The hidden Ulster lies beneath.
        A sudden blow, she collapsed with
        The other island; and the South
                's been made a cuckold.
        She has had family by them both,
                She's growing old

25   And scared that both have turned against her.
       The cuckold's impotent in Leinster
       House. The party in Westminster,
            All passion spent,
       More down-and-out than sinister,
            Just pays the rent.

26   Exhaustion underlies the scene.
       In Kensington, on Stephen's Green,
       The slogans have all ceased to mean
            Or almost ceased—
       Ulster is British is a tune
            Not quite deceased

27   In Ulster, though on "the mainland"—
       Cf., above, "the other island"—
       Ulster is part of Paddyland,
            And Londonderry
       Is far away as New England
            Or County Kerry.

28   So let's not raise a big hubbub.
       Steer between Scylla and Charyb
       A middle way that's neither glib
            Nor apocalyptic,
       Suggested by the poet Holub
            In his Aesopic

29   Fable of proper naming, set
       In a cinema: a man yells out
       When a beaver's called a muskrat
            By the narrator,
       Some Actors' Union hack, no doubt,
            Dubbed in later

30　On footage of the beaver dam —
　　Your usual, B-feature flim-flam.
　　Anyhow, as the creature swam
　　　　　And built and gnawed,
　　This man breaks out into a spasm
　　　　　Of constant, loud

31　And unembarrassed protestation.
　　Names were not for negotiation.
　　Right names were the first foundation
　　　　　For telling truth.
　　The audience, all irritation,
　　　　　Cries "Shut your mouth!

32　"Does he have to spoil our evening out?
　　Who is this self-promoting lout?
　　Is it an epileptic bout?
　　　　　Muskrat? Who cares?
　　Get the manager. Get him out.
　　　　　To hell with beavers!"

33　Need I go on? I hate to bite
　　Hands that led me to the limelight
　　In the Penguin book, I regret
　　　　　The awkwardness.
　　But British, no, the name's not right.
　　　　　Yours truly, Seamus.

NOTES

Stanza 1   This open letter is prompted by the writer's inclusion in *The Penguin Book of Contemporary British Poetry*, edited by Blake Morrison and Andrew Motion, Harmondsworth, 1982. I have to apologize for changing the *Poetry* of the title to *verse* — a result of the constrictions of rhyme.

Stanza 8   "Good advocate". Blake Morrison is the author of a critical study, *Seamus Heaney,* in Methuen's Contemporary Writers series, London, 1982.

Stanza 9   *Opened Ground* is a quotation from "Glanmore Sonnets, 1" in the writer's *Field Work,* London, 1979.

Stanza 10   References to reviews of the Penguin anthology by Philip Larkin, Hugh Haughton and John Jordan in *The Observer, Times Literary Supplement,* and *Irish Press* respectively.

Stanza 20   See Donald Davie, "Poet: Patriot: Interpreter," *Critical Inquiry,* Volume 9, Number 1, Chicago, 1982.

Stanza 28   See Miroslav Holub's "On the Necessity of Truth," in *Saggital Section,* translated by Stuart Frieberg and Dana Habova, Ohio, 1980.

Civilians and Barbarians

by Seamus Deane

Seamus Deane Graduate of Queen's University, Belfast and Cambridge University. Member of the Royal Irish Academy, Professor of English and American Literature at University College, Dublin. Woodrow Wilson Fellow and Fulbright Scholar at Reed College, Oregon, USA. Visiting Professor at University of California, Berkeley and University of Notre Dame, Indiana, USA.

Has published extensively on a wide variety of topics in English, French and Irish literature. Publications include: poetry — *Gradual Wars* (1972), *Rumours* (1977), *History Lessons* (1983); criticism — *Celtic Revivals* (1985). Forthcoming publications: *A Short History of Irish Writing 1580-1980, France and England 1789-1832.*

Winner of A.E. Memorial Award for Literature, 1973.
A Director of Field Day.

3

CIVILIANS AND BARBARIANS

Those who live under the law are civilians; those who live beyond it are barbarians. "Law makes men free in the political arena, just as reason makes men free in the universe as a whole".[1] Barbarians, therefore, are slaves, since they live in a world from which the operation of arbitrary individual will has not been eliminated. Law compels men to be free. In this paradox is to be found the nucleus of modern European theories of freedom, from Locke to Rousseau and beyond. But it was a common conception long before it received its articulation as an integral element in a comprehensive political philosophy. Nicholas Canny has provided us with an analysis of the background to Edmund Spenser's *View of the Present State of Ireland* (1596) which demonstrates the prevalence of the notion that the Irish must be compelled to be free by a sustained policy of war followed by good government. One John Davies, for instance, is quoted as saying in his *Discovery of the True Causes why Ireland was Never Entirely Subdued* (1612) that

> ... the husbandman must first break the land before it be made capable of good seed: and when it is thoroughly broken and manured, if he do not forthwith cast good seed into it, it will grow wild again, and bear nothing but weeds. So a barbarous country must be first broken by war before it will be capable of good government; and when it is fully subdued and conquered, if it be not well planted and governed after the conquest, it will eftsoons return to the former barbarism.[2]

To become free and prosperous the Irish were evidently going to have to become English. Spenser had objected to the Irish habit of abusing the English system of common law by presenting false evidence or producing unfair verdicts because

---

1 John Locke, *Two Treaties of Government* edited and introduced by Peter Laslett, (Cambridge, 1960), p. 111.

2 Nicholas Canny, "Edmund Spenser and the Development of an Anglo-Irish Identity" *The Yearbook of English Studies* vol. 13 (1983), pp. 1-19. Quoted, p. 15.

their loyalty was to their system of clan kinship and not to
English law. Thus he suggested that the Irish septs be dissolved,
that the Irish be moved into the towns, mingled with the
settlers, educated in English, in grammar and in science

> . . . whereby they will in short time grow up to that civil
> conversation that both the children will loathe the former
> rudeness in which they were bred, and also their parents
> will, even by the ensample of their young children,
> perceive the foulness of their own brutish behaviour
> compared to theirs, for learning hath that wonderful
> power of itself that it can soften and temper the most stern
> and savage nature.[3]

The failure of this policy in succeeding centuries led
Coleridge to contemplate with some horror the rise in Ireland
of a new species of patriotism in the guise of the United
Irishmen as a "delusive and pernicious sublimation of local
predilection and clannish pride, into a sentiment and principle
of nationality".[4] Writing in 1814, Coleridge gives a brief
account of the failure of English policy in Ireland since the days
of Henry II up to the achievement of legislative independence
in 1782 and thence to the Union and the United Irishmen. In
his reading of the story, he echoes Spenser's complaint that the
English government policy was never sufficiently sustained;
that it was concessive only under pressure and that it was now
faced with a species of local patriotism which, though far
removed from the real thing, was nevertheless extremely
dangerous. The danger arose from three sources. First, many
supporters of Irish patriotism believed that

> . . . they were labouring as the pioneers of civilization; and
> that political zealotry was calculated to act on Protestant-
> ism and Papistry, with all their Irish accretions, as an
> alkali on water and oil; and though caustic and corrosive
> in its own nature, unite the two incongruous natures into a
> milky and cleansing quality, that would remove from the
> moral countenance of Ireland all the anger-spots and
> efflorescences produced by intestine heats.[5]

Second, there was the Irish predilection for foreign
connections, through the Church, with its clergy educated
abroad, and through the Catholic gentry's preference for
foreign military service. Third, were all those circumstances

---

3   Ibid. p. 6.

4   *The Collected Works of Samuel Taylor Coleridge, Essays on His Times* ed
    D.V. Erdman, vol. II, p. 411.

5   Ibid. II, pp. 412-13.

. . . which makes the population of Ireland, at once the most numerous, and with few exceptions, the least civilized of Christian Europe, with fewer gradations and modes of interdependence; with less descending influence of opinions and manners from the gentry of the country; but above all, *with a more confirmed habit of obeying powers not constituted or acknowledged by the laws and Government, and of course with as much greater devotion as conscience is mightier than law.*[6]

Although Coleridge characteristically failed to complete his account of the Irish situation on the eve of Waterloo, his journalistic writings on the topic retain many of the features of his seventeenth century predecessors. Most pronounced among these are the assumption that the strife in Ireland is the consequence of a battle between English civilization, based on laws, and Irish barbarism, based on local kinship loyalties and sentiments; that the added complication of religion helps to intensify that Irish barbarism by fostering ignorance and sloth, disrespect for English law and respect for Papal decrees in its stead, conspiracy and rebellion by cherishing foreign connections hostile to England. The one marked difference Coleridge notices in 1814 is the claim by the United Irishmen that their patriotism will subdue religious differences by substituting the common name of Irishman for that of Catholic or Dissenter. He did, therefore, see the significance of what Tone represented but he feared that the development of what he called 'local patriotism' among what he had described in 1800 as "the vindictive turbulence of a wild and barbarous race, brutalised by the oppression of centuries"[7] would turn into a Jacobin rebellion, leading to the separation of the two islands. That would never do.

The wisdom of English commentators on Irish affairs has always been vitiated by the assumption that there is some undeniable relationship between civilization, the Common Law and Protestantism. Ireland has remained a permanent rebuke to this assumption, and has been subjected to vilification on that account. The assumption has remained unquestioned. But Ireland has not been alone in this matter. The English interpretation of the French Revolution was governed for the first thirty years of the nineteenth century by the belief that the French had failed to do in 1789 what the English had done in 1688 because, being Catholics (lapsed or otherwise), and therefore acclimatised to despotism and the operations of arbitrary

---

6   Ibid. p. 413 (my emphasis in the last lines).
7   Ibid. I. p. 106.

rule, they were unfit for liberty. This argument has been produced over and over again, *mutatis mutandis,* to deny freedom to colonial peoples. It seems a little odd to see it used by one colonial power against another. Those who, like Hazlitt, would have liked to see the Revolution, led by Napoleon, over-throw Legitimacy, did not have to look far to discover why the French failed to support their great Emperor.

> Perhaps a reformation in religion ought always to precede a revolution in the government. Catholics may make good subjects, but bad rebels. They are so used to the trammels of authority, that they do not immediately know how to do without them; or, like manumitted slaves, only feel assured of their liberty in committing some Saturnalian license. A revolution, to give it stability and soundness, should first be conducted down to a Protestant ground.[8]

Commentators of a far more virulent Francophobia than Hazlitt's produced scores of essays and pamphlets in which the new French revolutionary philosophy was described as "barbarous" and its supporters as every species of wretch and miscreant. In 1793, Horace Walpole, having exhausted his considerable powers of invective, decided that the French deserved nothing more than their own name.

> But I have no words that can reach the criminality of such *inferno-human* beings — but must compose a term that aims at conveying my idea of them — for the future it will be sufficient to call them *the French.*[9]

More than twenty years later, Robert Southey, the friend of Coleridge and Wordsworth, and one-time radical, announced in the course of a defence of the English alliance between Church and State:

> If a breach be made in our sanctuary, it will be by the combined forces of Popery, Dissent, and Unbelief, fighting under a political flag.[10]

The threat to the English sanctuary was, in short, nationalism of the French revolutionary sort. The dispute between barbarism and civilization had by now undergone a transformation. Races like the French and the Irish, in their

---

8 *The Complete Works of William Hazlitt* ed. P.P. Howe, 21 vols., (London 1930-34), vol. 13, (*The Life of Napoleon Buonaparte,* written 1828-30), p. 56.

9 *The Correspondence of Horace Walpole* ed. W.S. Lewis XXXI (New Haven, 1961), p. 377.

10 Robert Southey, *Sir Thomas More: or, Colloquies on the Progress and Prospects of Society* 2 vols. (London, 1829), II, p. 43.

resistance to the English idea of liberty, had now become criminalised — *inferno-human* beings. As evangelicalism in England rose through the social system from the Methodists to the Anglicans, the specifically Protestant resistance to the characteristic sins of these races became more pronounced. In the case of the French, the sin was lasciviousness; in the case of the Irish, it was drunkenness. Neither was 'manly'; both were symptoms of a deep corruption; the corruption was itself a failure in self-discipline and respect for law, moral or positive. The profile of the frigidly sober English Victorian disciplinarian emerged against the political background of the old quarrels between France and England, Ireland and England, civilisation (with all its discontents) and barbarism (with all its 'lewde libertie').[11]

The complicated history of the various temperance movements in Irish history and their connections with nationalist and anti-nationalist ideologies reveals the deep disquiet felt among many sects and classes about the social manifestations of Irish 'barbarism'.[12] When the movements were led by Protestant evangelicals, their aim was to extirpate the disease by introducing preventive legislation. The various licensing acts of the nineteenth century are their monument and Ian Paisley's recent defence (February, 1983) of the Northern Irish Sabbath as a tourist attraction their most recent echo. When led by Catholic Churchmen, like Father Mathew in Ireland or Cardinal Manning among the Irish in England, their aim was to promote abstinence, not by law, but by conscience. This distinction shows a curious reversal of the conventional Protestant/Catholic attitudes. In Ireland, the Protestant has tended to turn to law and the State even in matters of social and moral attitude, because Protestantism and the State have been for so long in a defensive alliance with one another. The Catholic, on the other hand, has turned to conscience and the Church (increasingly the same thing in the modern period), seeking from the Church rather than the State legitimisation for social and moral issues. The temperance movement in the nineteenth century was one of the signs of the Catholic Church's increasing authority in areas which, before the Famine, had not been open to its discipline. However temperance was only one of a series of social movements which had increased civility and respectability among the masses of the people as its aim.

---

11 A phrase from Spenser's *View of the Present State of Ireland.*
12 See Elizabeth Malcolm, "Temperance and Irish Nationalism" in *Ireland Under the Union* ed. F.S.L. Lyons and R.A.J. Hawkins (Oxford, 1980), pp. 69-114.

The attachment of the stigma of criminality to drinking, especially among the poor, was a symptom of the increasingly coercive function of law as an instrument for extending efficiency and order in a society where waste and disorder were rampant. The various State-run enterprises in nineteenth century Ireland — in health, through the dispensary system; in education, through the national schools; in cartography through the Ordnance Survey; in policing, through the establishment, by 1836, of a nationally controlled para-military force; in law, through the system of Resident Magistrates — had a highly Spenserian aim in view — the civilisation of the wild natives.[13] All of these schemes were, in effect, pieces of preventive legislation. A whole range of conditions — like the condition of being drunk, or illiterate, or from somewhere unheard of or unknown, or vagrant, or disaffected — was now realised as being beyond (not exactly against) the law. As with certain laws in England, like the Vagrancy Act of 1824, an imputed intention or reputation was, *in itself*, criminal. Section 4 of that Act criminalised "every suspected person or reputed thief" who frequented the dockland areas of industrial England.[14] Such legislation need a developed police force for its implementation. In Ireland, the police force was far more advanced than in England. The legislation was far more draconian and politically directed. Because of the recurrent agrarian unrest and the political disturbances Insurrection Acts, Arms Acts and Peace Preservation Acts stand "like monuments to misrule in the years between the Act of Union and the Famine".[15]

Thus, in the nineteenth century, a new State-controlled system of education, police, preventive law, health, prison, workhouse, ordnance maps, emerged to provide that sustained governmental policy which the seventeenth century colonisers had sought from Whitehall. In Ireland, the coercive legislation was especially prominent but its aim, while more blatant, was no different. This was to suppress a condition of mind. After all, in 1867, the Manchester martyrs were hanged on the same evidence as had led to the pardon and release of an innocent bystander, Maguire. "The implied attitude in the home secretary's discrimination was that Maguire had shown no

13 See Oliver MacDonagh, *Ireland, the Union and its Aftermath* (London, 1977), ch. 2.
14 I am indebted to an unpublished article by Barry McAuley of the Faculty of Law at UCD for this information and some of these ideas. The article is titled, "The Grammar of Western Criminal Justice".
15 George Dangerfield, *The Damnable Question: A Study in Anglo-Irish Relations* (London, 1977), p. 9.

38

animosity to the authority of the queen and deserved to live, while the rest took pride in their Irish attitudes and deserved to die".[16] That condition of mind was not necessarily Irish. It was the condition of *homo criminalis*, the criminal type, that theoretical construct of the great age of scientific criminology, the detective novel and high industrial capitalism. The Irish mind, or certain conditions thereof, was, to the English mind, in most conditions thereof, ineluctably criminal because of the very simple fact that it tended to show remarkably consistent disrespect for English law and, therefore (!) for the Law as such. The stereotypes of the Irish person — the quaint Paddy or the simian terrorist — arise quite naturally from the conviction that there are criminal types, politically as well as socially identifiable to the police and to all decent citizens. Conrad's *The Secret Agent* (1907), with its expert conflation of Fenian and Russian anarchist stereotypes, is the most memorable of all anti-revolutionary and anti-terrorist fictions, with the outrage at its heart being the attempt to blow up Greenwich Mean Time itself with a bomb unwittingly carried by an idiot. Spenserian barbarism, transmuted into professional anarchism (or, as we would say, international terrorism) has now the organised police force and organised time and space as its civilized enemy.

This brings us to the doorstep of our own time. The language of politics in Ireland and England, especially when the subject is Northern Ireland, is still dominated by the putative division between barbarism and civilization. Civilization still defines itself as a system of law; and it defines barbarism (which, by the nature of the distinction, cannot be capable of defining itself), as a chaos of arbitrary wills, an Hobbesian state of nature. But it is a distinction which operates within a modern state system which prides itself on the transparency of the whole population to the concentrated stare of bureaucratic (including police and military) control. In Ireland, this new situation (dating from the early nineteenth century) has enormously increased the ideological rift between the competing discourses of the civilian and the barbarian. For the romantic nationalism which was born in that utilitarian century gave to certain aspects of 'barbarism' a privileged status. In literature, for instance, 'barbarism' became 'primitivism' and represented a vigour lost to the sophisticated art of the civilised world. On the other hand, the same nationalism insisted on the high degree of civilisation it had attained socially, although in some of the temperance debates

16 Malcolm Brown, *The Politics of Irish Literature* (Seattle, 1972), p. 209.

both O'Connell and Davis give us a version of Irish life which seems to have been modelled on some of the more saccharine passages in Dickens. The essential issues have, however, been 'displaced' into literature in such a manner that their reality has been further attenuated in the minds of the Irish people. The writer as barbarian, the audience as civilian — that is an easily accepted exercise in role playing. But the romanticisation of writing involved in this is not nearly so important as the humiliating conquest of the audience. For such an audience is tamed; it has learned to be submissive to the massive system of controls which the modern political machine operates. Among those systems of control is the image of the writer as licensed barbarian — a sort of wild Irish native performing in an English court. But, beyond that, there is the much more concentrated manipulation of the civilian audience's reaction to the other kind of outsider — the criminal type and, above all, the *politically* criminal type, your friendly neighbourhood terrorist.

This stereotype has all the classic faults of the barbarian as seen from the view of the English civilian. First he is Irish; next Catholic; and, if not Catholic, then an extreme Protestant, a Dissenter of the old, troublesome Calvinistic or Ranter type; in addition he is from a working-class background and is unemployed (unemployable); therefore he draws money from the benevolent state which he intends to subvert and by which he is oppressed as he was also educated and fed free milk by it. He is from an area of dirt and desolation, not to be equalled in Western Europe, a blot on the fair face of the United Kingdom. He drinks a lot for, since the Fenians, it has been a standard piece of English lore that all Irish guerilla groups meet in pubs when they are not blowing them up. Sometimes, they manage to do both. Finally, and worst of all, he is sometimes a she. Locked in a poverty trap, lost in a mist of sentiment and nostalgia, exploiting the safeguards of laws they despise, faithful to codes other than those of the English rite, they are the perfect reproduction, with some nineteenth century romantic tints, of Spenser's wild Irish. Most important of all, they are not only barbarians, they are criminals. Their opponents, who wear uniforms, and live in barracks, and drive armoured cars, operate checkpoints, etc. etc., kill with impunity, because they represent, they embody the Law. The terrorist embodies its denial. The brutal exploitation of events by both sides demonstrates over and over again the endlessness of the battle for supremacy of one kind of discourse, one set of political attitudes over another.

This is plain enough. But complications set in — as in an

illness — when modes of discourse other than the political become involved. The moral mode, much favoured of course by the Churches, although not ignored in the least by either governments, armies or the media, has a distorting effect on the political realities involved. For it is based (however hypocritically) on the notion of an immutable Natural Law, or Moral Code, the peremptory force of which applies more directly to the terrorist than to the soldier of the State. There is an interesting political distinction between the appeals made by clergy to terrorists and those made to the forces of Law and Order. The first are made to individuals, loners, to come in out of the moral cold, to cease disgracing the cause they ostensibly represent; the second are made to a corporate body, not to the individual. The 'barbarians' are always 'men and women', or specific, even named, individuals. They enjoy the privilege of individuality precisely because they will not be granted the status of a corporate force within civil society. The ground of the appeal, however, is that of the universal condition of mankind, redeemed and unredeemed, saved and damned, or, if you like, civilian and barbarian. The moral and religious idiom, which claims this universality, has in fact been incorporated into the political idiom which *appears* to be more local in its range. The moral idiom therefore is no more than a reinforcement of the political while appearing to be independent of it. The systematic nature of political and moral idioms, the organic coherence conferred upon them by the prevalence of political interests, makes the distinction between them suspect. Nothing demonstrated this more than the Peace Movement, one of the most successful of all political exploitations of a moral code which was in fact a political code. Hardly anyone remembers that the incident which sparked the movement off began with the killing of an IRA man, who was driving a car, by a British soldier — who was himself in no danger. The charismatic movement in Catholicism and the evangelical movement in Protestantism combined to display, in front of the cameras, the longing for peace by a population disturbed by the guerillas within their ranks — not by the army, or the police, or the unemployment, housing conditions and so forth. As farces go, it was one of the most successful of modern times.

But it was an important success. For it changed nothing. Therefore it was a success for the State. It merely confirmed and spread the demonising mythology. Later, the dirty protest at the Maze was to supply it with the most horrific imagery of degradation, although the conspiracy between the degraded and the degraders became so close at that time that the filthy nakedness of the prisoners and the space-suited automatism of the disinfecting jailers seemed to be an agreed contrast in their respective images of what they represented — vulnerable Irish squalor, impervious, impersonal English decontamination. That changed nothing either. Nor did the hunger strikes, although for a time it seemed as if they might change everything. The point of crisis was passed without anyone seeming to know why the explosion did not come. Perhaps the truth is that both sides had played out their self-appointed roles to such a literal end, that there was nothing left but the sense of exhaustion. Political languages fade more slowly than literary languages but when they do, they herald a deep structural alteration in the attitudes which sustain a crisis. Of all the blighting distinctions which govern our responses and limit our imaginations at the moment, none is more potent than this four hundred year-old distinction between barbarians and civilians. We may ask, with Bishop Berkeley in *The Querist*

> Whether the natural phlegm of this island needs any additional stupefier?

Heroic Styles : the tradition of an idea

by Seamus Deane

4

HEROIC STYLES:
THE TRADITION OF AN IDEA

It is possible to write about literature without adverting in any substantial way to history. Equally, it is possible to write history without any serious reference to literature. Yet both literature and history are discourses which are widely recognised to be closely related to one another because they are both subject to various linguistic protocols which, in gross or in subtle ways, determine the structure and meaning of what is written. We have many names for these protocols. Some are very general indeed—Romanticism, Victorianism, Modernism. Some are more specific — Idealist, Radical, Liberal. Literature can be written as History, History as Literature. It would be foolhardy to choose one among the many competing variations and say that it is *true* on some specifically historical or literary basis. Such choices are always moral and/or aesthetic. They always have an ideological implication.

Similarly, both discourses are surrounded — some would say stifled — by what is now called metacommentary. History as an activity is interrogated by the philosophy of history; literature as an activity is scrutinised by literary criticism which, at times, manages to be the philosophy of literature. In Ireland, however, the two discourses have been kept apart, even though they have, between them, created the interpretations of past and present by which we live. It is always possible to see in retrospect the features which identify writers of a particular period, no matter how disparate their interests. The link between Yeats, Spengler and Toynbee is obvious by now. They all speak the language of a particular historical 'family'. The same is true of Joyce and Lukács. What I propose in this pamphlet is that there have been for us two dominant ways of reading both our literature and our history. One is 'Romantic', a mode of reading which takes pleasure in the notion that Ireland is a culture enriched by the ambiguity of its relationship to an anachronistic and a modernised present. The other is a mode of reading which denies the glamour of this ambiguity and seeks to escape from it into a pluralism of the present. The authors who represent these modes most powerfully are Yeats and Joyce respectively. The problem which is rendered insoluble by them is that of the North. In a basic sense, the crisis we are passing through is stylistic. That is to say, it is a crisis of language — the ways in which we write it and the ways in which we read it.

The idea of a tradition is one with which we are familiar in Irish writing. In a culture like ours, 'tradition' is not easily taken to be an established reality. We are conscious that it is an invention, a narrative which ingeniously finds a way of connect-ing a selected series of historical figures or themes in such a way that the pattern or plot revealed to us becomes a conditioning factor in our reading of literary works — such as *The Tower* or *Finnegans Wake*. However, the paradox into which we are inevitably led has a disquieting effect, for then we recognise that a Yeatsian or a Joycean idea of tradition is something simultaneously established for us in their texts and as a pre-condition of being able to read them. A poem like "Ancestral Houses" owes its force to the vitality with which it offers a version of Ascendancy history as true in itself. The truth of this historical reconstruction of the Ascendancy is not cancelled by our simply saying No, it was not like that. For its ultimate validity is not historical, but mythical. In this case, the mythical element is given prominence by the meditation on the fate of an originary energy when it becomes so effective that it transforms nature into civilization and is then transformed itself by civilization into decadence. This poem, then, appears to have a story to tell and, along with that, an interpretation of the story's meaning. It operates on the narrative and on the conceptual planes and at the intersection of these it emerges, for many readers, as a poem about the tragic nature of human existence itself. Yeats's life, through the mediations of history and myth, becomes an embodiment of essential existence.

The trouble with such a reading is the assumption that this or any other literary work can arrive at a moment in which it takes leave of history or myth (which are liable to idiosyncratic interpretation) and becomes meaningful only as an aspect of the 'human condition'. This is, of course, a characteristic determination of humanist readings of literature which hold to the ideological conviction that literature, in its highest forms, is non-ideological. It would be perfectly appropriate, within this particular frame, to take a poem by Pearse — say, *The Rebel* — and to read it in the light of a story — the Republican tradition from Tone, the Celtic tradition from Cuchulainn, the Christian tradition from Colmcille — and then reread the story as an expression of the moral supremacy of martyrdom over oppression. But as a poem, it would be regarded as inferior to that of Yeats. Yeats, stimulated by the moribund state of the Ascendancy tradition, resolves, on the level of literature, a crisis which, for him, cannot be resolved socially or politically. In Pearse's case, the poem is no more than an adjunct to political action. The revolutionary tradition he represents is not broken by oppression but renewed by it. His symbols survive outside the poem, in the Cuchulainn statue, in the reconstituted GPO, in the military behaviour and rhetoric of the IRA. Yeats's symbols have disappeared, the destruction of Coole Park being the most notable, although even in their disappearance one can discover reinforcement for the tragic condition embodied in the poem. The unavoidable fact about both poems is that they continue to belong to history and to myth; they are part of the symbolic procedures which characterise their culture. Yet, to the extent that we prefer one as literature to the other, we find ourselves inclined to dispossess it of history, to concede to it an autonomy which is finally defensible only on the grounds of style.

The consideration of style is a thorny problem. In Irish writing, it is particularly so. When the language is English, Irish writing is dominated by the notion of vitality restored, of the centre energised by the periphery, the urban by the rural, the cosmopolitan by the provincial, the decadent by the natural. This is one of the liberating effects of nationalism, a means of restoring dignity and power to what had been humiliated and suppressed. This is the idea which underlies all our formulations of tradition. Its development is confined to two variations. The first we may call the variation of adherence, the second of separation. In the first, the restoration of native energy to the English language is seen as a specifically Irish contribution to a shared heritage. Standard English, as a form of language or as a form of literature, is rescued from its exclusiveness by being compelled to incorporate into itself what had previously been regarded as a delinquent dialect. It is the Irish contribution, in literary terms, to the treasury of English verse and prose. Cultural nationalism is thus transformed into a species of literary unionism. Sir Samuel Ferguson is the most explicit supporter of this variation, although, from Edgeworth to Yeats, it remains a tacit assumption. The story of the spiritual heroics of a fading class — the Ascendancy — in the face of a transformed Catholic 'nation' — was rewritten in a variety of ways in literature — as the story of the pagan Fianna replaced by a pallid Christianity, of young love replaced by old age (Deirdre, Oisin), of aristocracy supplanted by mob-democracy. The fertility of these rewritings is all the more remarkable in that they were recruitments by the fading class of the myths of renovation which belonged to their opponents. Irish culture became the new property of those who were losing their grip on Irish land. The effect of these rewritings was to transfer the blame for the drastic condition of the country from the Ascendancy to the Catholic middle classes or to their English counterparts. It was in essence a strategic retreat from political to cultural supremacy. From Lecky to Yeats and forward to F.S.L. Lyons we witness the conversion of Irish history into a tragic theatre in which the great Anglo-Irish protagonists — Swift, Burke, Parnell — are destroyed in their heroic attempts to unite culture of intellect with the emotion of multitude, or, in political terms, constitutional politics with the forces of revolution. The triumph of the forces of revolution is glossed in all cases as the success of a philistine modernism over a rich and integrated organic culture. Yeats's promiscuity in his courtship of heroic figures — Cuchulainn, John O'Leary, Parnell, the 1916 leaders, Synge, Mussolini, Kevin O'Higgins, General O'Duffy — is an understandable form of anxiety in one who sought to find in a single figure the capacity to give reality to a spiritual leadership for which (as he consistently admitted) the conditions had already disappeared. Such figures could only operate as symbols. Their significance lay in their disdain for the provincial, squalid aspects of a mob culture which is the Yeatsian version of the other face of Irish nationalism. It could provide him culturally with a language of renovation, but it provided neither art nor civilization. That had come, politically, from the connection between England and Ireland.

All the important Irish Protestant writers of the nineteenth century had, as the ideological centre of their work, a commitment to a minority or subversive attitude which was much less revolutionary than it appeared to be. Edgeworth's critique of landlordism was counterbalanced by her sponsorship of utilitarianism and "British manufacturers";[1] Maturin and Le Fanu took the sting out of Gothicism by allying it with an ethic of aristocratic loneliness; Shaw and Wilde denied the subversive force of their proto-socialism by expressing it as cosmopolitan wit, the recourse of the social or intellectual dandy who makes

---

[1] The phrase is from the penultimate sentence of *Castle Rackrent* (1800):

It is a problem difficult of solution to determine, whether an Union will hasten or retard the amelioration of this country. The few gentlemen of education who now reside in this country will resort to England: they are few, but they are in nothing inferior to men of the same rank in Great Britain. The best that can happen will be the introduction of British manufacturers in their places.

On Maria Edgeworth's reluctance to accept fully the idea of an Irish Catholic gentleman, see the comments by Stephen Gwynn in *Irish Literature and Drama in the English Language: A Short History* (London, 1936) pp.54-6.

such a fetish of taking nothing seriously that he ceases to be taken seriously himself. Finally, Yeats's preoccupation with the occult, and Synge's with the lost language of Ireland are both minority positions which have, as part of their project, the revival of worn social forms, not their overthrow. The disaffection inherent in these positions is typical of the Anglo-Irish criticism of the failure of English civilization in Ireland, but it is articulated for an English audience which learned to regard all these adversarial positions as essentially picturesque manifestations of the Irish sensibility. In the same way, the Irish mode of English was regarded as picturesque too and when both language and ideology are rendered harmless by this view of them, the writer is liable to become a popular success. Somerville and Ross showed how to take the middle-class seriousness out of Edgeworth's world and make it endearingly quaint. But all nineteenth-century Irish writing exploits the connection between the picturesque and the popular. In its comic vein, it produces *The Shaughran* and *Experiences of an Irish R.M.*; in its Gothic vein, *Melmoth the Wanderer, Uncle Silas* and *Dracula*; in its mandarin vein, the plays of Wilde and the poetry of the young Yeats. The division between that which is picturesque and that which is useful did not pass unobserved by Yeats. He made the great realignment of the minority stance with the pursuit of perfection in art. He gave the picturesque something more than respectability. He gave it the mysteriousness of the esoteric and in doing so committed Irish writing to the idea of an art which, while belonging to 'high' culture, would not have, on the one hand, the asphyxiating decadence of its English or French counterparts and, on the other hand, would have within it the energies of a community which had not yet been reduced to a public. An idea of art opposed to the idea of utility, an idea of an audience opposed to the idea of popularity, an idea of the peripheral becoming the central culture — in these three ideas Yeats provided Irish writing with a programme for action. But whatever its connection with Irish nationalism, it was not, finally, a programme of separation from the English tradition. His continued adherence to it led him to define the central Irish attitude as one of self-hatred. In his extraordinary "A General Introduction for my Work" (1937), he wrote:

> The 'Irishry' have preserved their ancient 'deposit' through wars which, during the sixteenth and seventeenth centuries, became wars of extermination; no people, Lecky said . . . have undergone greater persecution, nor did that persecution altogether cease up to our own day. No people hate as we do in whom that past is always alive . . . Then I

remind myself that though mine is the first English marriage I know of in the direct line, all my family names are English, and that I owe my soul to Shakespeare, to Spenser and to Blake, perhaps to William Morris, and to the English language in which I think, speak, and write, that everything I love has come to me through English; my hatred tortures me with love, my love with hate . . . This is Irish hatred and solitude, the hatred of human life that made Swift write *Gulliver* and the epitaph upon his tomb, that can still make us wag between extremes and doubt our sanity.

The pathology of literary unionism has never been better defined.

The second variation in the development of the idea of vitality restored is embodied most perfectly in Joyce. His work is dominated by the idea of separation as a means to the revival of suppressed energies. The separation he envisages is as complete as one could wish. The English literary and political imperium, the Roman Catholic and Irish nationalist claims, the oppressions of conventional language and of conventional narrative — all of these are overthrown, but the freedom which results is haunted by his fearful obsession with treachery and betrayal. In him, as in many twentieth century writers, the natural ground of vitality is identified as the libidinal. The sexual forms of oppression are inscribed in all his works but, with that, there is also the ambition to see the connection between sexuality and history. His work is notoriously preoccupied with paralysis, inertia, the disabling effects of society upon the individual who, like Bloom, lives within its frame, or, like Stephen, attempts to live beyond it. In *Portrait* the separation of the aesthetic ambition of Stephen from the political, the sexual and the religious zones of experience is clear. It is, of course, a separation which includes them, but as oppressed forces which were themselves once oppressive. His comment on Wilde is pertinent:

> Here we touch the pulse of Wilde's art — sin. He deceived himself into believing that he was the bearer of good news of neo-paganism to an enslaved people . . . But if some truth adheres . . . to his restless thought . . . at its very base is the truth inherent in the soul of Catholicism: that man cannot reach the divine heart except through that sense of separation and loss called sin.[2]

In Joyce himself the sin is treachery, sexual or political infidelity.

---

[2] James Joyce, *The Critical Writings* ed. E. Mason and R. Ellmann (New York, 1964) pp.204-5.

The betrayed figure is the alien artist. The 'divine heart' is the maternal figure, mother, Mother Ireland, Mother Church or Mother Eve. But the betrayed are also the betrayers and the source of the treachery is in the Irish condition itself. In his Trieste lecture of 1907, "Ireland, Island of Saints and Sages", he notes that Ireland was betrayed by her own people and by the Vatican on the crucial occasions of Henry II's invasion and the Act of Union.

> From my point of view, these two facts must be thoroughly explained before the country in which they occurred has the most rudimentary right to persuade one of her sons to change his position from that of an unprejudiced observer to that of a convicted nationalist.[3]

Finally, in his account of the Maamtrasna murders of 1882 in "Ireland at the Bar" (published in *Il Piccolo della Sera,* Trieste, 1907), Joyce, anticipating the use which he would make throughout *Finnegans Wake* of the figure of the Irish-speaking Myles Joyce, judicially murdered by the sentence of an English-speaking court, comments

> The figure of this dumbfounded old man, a remnant of a civilization not ours, deaf and dumb before his judge, is a symbol of the Irish nation at the bar of public opinion.[4]

This, along with the well-known passage from *Portrait* in which Stephen feels the humiliation of being alien to the English language in the course of his conversation with the Newman-Catholic Dean of Studies, identifies Joyce's sense of separation from both Irish and English civilisation. Betrayed into alienation, he turns to art to enable him overcome the treacheries which have victimised him.

In one sense, Joyce's writing is founded on the belief in the capacity of art to restore a lost vitality. So the figures we remember are embodiments of this 'vitalism', particularly Molly Bloom and Anna Livia Plurabelle. The fact that they were women is important too, since it clearly indicates some sort of resolution, on the level of femaleness, of what had remained implacably unresolvable on the male level, whether that be of Stephen and Bloom or of Shem and Shaun. This vitalism announces itself also in the protean language of these books, in their endless transactions between history and fiction, macro- and microcosm. But along with this, there is in Joyce a

---

[3]   *Critical Writings* pp.162-3.

[4]   *CW* p.198 On his use of this incident in *Finnegans Wake,* see John Garvin, *James Joyce's Disunited Kingdom and the Irish Dimension* (Dublin, 1976), pp.163-9.

recognition of a world which is 'void' (a favourite word of his), even though it is also full of correspondence, objects, people. His registration of the detail of Dublin life takes 'realism' to the point of parody, takes the sequence of items which form a plot into the series of items which form an inventory. The clean and clinical detail of *Dubliners* is akin to what he speaks of in his essay on Blake, where he describes Michelangelo's influence on the poet as evinced in

> . . . the importance of the pure, clean line that evokes and creates the figure on the background of the uncreated void.[5]

His vitalism is insufficient to the task of overcoming this void. The inexhaustibility of his texts is a symptom of a social emptiness, of a world in which the subject, although one of culture's 'sons', is also 'an unprejudiced observer' whose view of any communal relationship — familial, political, religious — is darkened by the conviction that it is necessarily treacherous. The disenchantment with community in Joyce is not simply the denial by him or by a 'rational' Ulysses-like hero of myths, like nationalism or Catholicism. It is the disenchantment with privacy, especially with the heroic and privileged privacy of the individual consciousness, which is, in the end, the more disturbing discovery. The literary correlative of this is the replacement of the univocal, heroic, Yeatsian style with a polyglot mixture of styles (in *Ulysses*) and of languages (in *Finnegans Wake*). Yeats's various recuperations of 'aristocratic' and 'community' forms — though occult or occluded energies, from the 'Celtic' myths to the Japanese Noh play, from a 'national' theatre to the Blueshirt marching songs — are rebuked by Joyce's consumer-world, where the principle of connection is paratactic merely and the heroic artistic spirit is replaced by the trans-individual consciousness.

Yeats was indeed our last romantic in literature as was Pearse in politics. They were men who asserted a coincidence between the destiny of the community and their own and believed that this coincidence had an historical repercussion. This was the basis for their belief in a 'spiritual aristocracy' which worked its potent influence in a plebeian world. Their determination to restore vitality to this lost society provided their culture with a millenial conviction which has not yet died. Whatever we may think of their ideas of tradition, we still adhere to the tradition of the idea that art and revolution are definitively associated in their production of an individual style

[5]   *CW* p.221.

which is also the signature of the community's deepest self. The fascination with style has its roots in a tradition of opposition to official discourse, but, as we have seen, it leads to that vacillation between the extremes of picturesque caricature and tragic heroism which marks Irish literature and politics in the period since the Union. Since Swift, no major and few minor Irish writers have escaped this fate. Even Joyce, who repudiated the conditioning which made it inevitable, is subject to it. There is a profoundly insulting association in the secondary literature surrounding him that he is eccentric because of his Irishness but serious because of his ability to separate himself from it. In such judgements, we see the ghost of a rancid colonialism. But it is important to recognise that this ghost haunts the works themselves. The battle between style as the expression of communal history governed by a single imagination (as applicable to O'Connell, Parnell or De Valera as to Yeats or Synge) and Joycean stylism, in which the atomisation of community is registered in a multitude of equivalent, competing styles, in short, a battle between Romantic and contemporary Ireland. The terms of the dispute are outmoded but they linger on. The most obvious reason for this is the continuation of the Northern 'problem', where 'unionism' and 'nationalism' still compete for supremacy in relation to ideas of identity racially defined as either 'Irish' or 'British' in communities which are deformed by believing themselves to be the historic inheritors of those identities and the traditions presumed to go with them.

The narratives we have glanced at in the works of Joyce, Pearse and Yeats are all based on the ideological conviction that a community exists which must be recovered and restored. These communities — of the family in Joyce, of the Ascendancy in Yeats, of the revolutionary brotherhood in Pearse — underwent their restoration in literature which is self-consciously adversarial. Moreover, these narratives continue to send out their siren signals even though the crises they were designed to describe and overcome have long since disappeared. The signals have been at last picked up in Northern Ireland — for so long apparently immune to them — and are now being rebroadcast.

Both communities in the North pride themselves on being the lone and true inheritors of their respective traditions. Their vision of themselves is posited on this conviction of fidelity, even though this is slightly flawed by the simultaneous recognition that the fidelity might also be a product of isolation and provincialism. The Protestant self-image is closely bound up with the idea of liberty and with the image of the garrison. This is well-known, but within that there are the only slightly less well-known support images, of the elite people (sponsored both by Protestantism and by the exclusive Whig idea of liberty as a racial phenomenon) and of the lost tribe, adrift in the desert of the worldly and demonic. In opposition, the Catholic self-image is expressed in terms of the oppressed, the disowned, the aristocrat forced into the slum, the beseiger who attempts to break down the wall of prejudice which calls itself liberty. The stereotypes are easily recognised and their origins in history well-documented. Both communities cherish a millenial faith in the triumph of their own conceptions of right. For the Catholic, that means the disintegration of the State, for the Protestant that means its final preservation. Certain social concepts, like employment or housing, have an almost totem-istic significance in the reading both communities give to the British capitalist formation in which they are both enclosed. Discrimination in these areas against Catholics is for the Protestant, a variant of the garrison or siege mentality, of keeping them out. Instead of Derry's walls, we now have the shipyards or Shorts. The beseigers live in the perpetual ghetto of the permanently ominous, yet still permanently unsuccessful, environ. Within that, no less within a ghetto, lie the beseiged.

The spectacle is obviously pathological although, for all that, no less intimate with the social and political realities of the situation. The North has all the appearances of an abnormal, aberrant society. Yet it makes plainly manifest 'normal' injustices which are taken for granted elsewhere. The religious divide is not a disguised rendering of political and social divisions. It is, at one and the same time, an expression of them and, on a more intense level, a justification for them. No one denies the existence of serious injustices in the North. But there religion is given as the reason for them. This is true and false. It is true in that religion was introduced in the plantations and afterwards as a sectarian force. Whether the bible followed the sword, or the sword the bible, is irrelevant. They came, in effect, together. The very rationalisations produced to legitimise the conquest, also help to legitimise those injustices which still derive from it as well as those which are independent of it. The communities have become stereotyped into their roles of oppressor and victim to such an extent that the notion of a Protestant or a Catholic sensibility is now assumed to be a fact of nature rather than a product of these very special and ferocious conditions.

In such a situation, nothing is more likely to perpetuate and even galvanise these stereotypes than the dream of a community's attaining, through a species of spiritual-military heroics, its longed-for destiny. Each begins to seek, in such a climate, a leadership which will definitively embody the univocal style which is the expression of its inner essence or nature. But in such a confrontation, style is no less than a declaration of war. It is the annunciation of essence in a person, in a mode of behaviour, in a set of beliefs. Paisley, for example, is the most remarkable incarnation of the communal spirit of unionism. In him, violence, a trumpery evangelicalism, anti-popery and a craven adulation of the "British" way of life are soldered together in a populist return to the first principles of "Ulsterness". No other leader has the telluric power of this man. On the Catholic side, John Hume acts as the minority's agent of rational demystification and the IRA as its agency of millenial revenge. The cultural machinery of Romantic Ireland has so wholly taken over in the North that we have already seen in the last fifteen years the following characteristic paradigms repeated: — a literary efflorescence, ambiguously allied to the troubles; political theologies of 'armed struggle' and 'defence of the union'; the collapse of 'constitutionalism' in the face of British 'betrayal'; the emergence of an ancestral myth of origin, as in the work of Ian Adamson; hunger-strikes which achieve world prominence and give to the republican cause the rebel dignity it sought; the burning of Big Houses, attacks on barracks, a 'decent' British Army with some notorious berserk units — the Paras, the UDR. We have had all this before. What makes it different now is the widespread and probably justified conviction that this rerun is the last. That lends an air of desperation and boredom to the scene. Again, there is that recognisable vacillation between the picturesque and the tragic, between seeing the 'Northerner' in his full and overblown self-caricature and seeing in him the working out of a tragic destiny. The repetition of historical and literary paradigms is not necessarily farcical but there is an unavoidable tendency towards farce in a situation in which an acknowledged tragic conflict is also read as an anachronistic-aberrant-picturesque one. This reading conspires with the 'modern' interpretation of the North as a place undergoing in microcosm the international phenomenon of the battle of extremes between the terrorist and the rule of law, to restate the problem as a particularly unfortunate combination of both — a 'modern' problem deriving from an 'anachronistic' base.

But this is also the standard view of modern Irish writing, and one of the apparently inexplicable features of the Irish Revival. The appearance of what we may call an 'advanced' or 'modernist' literature in a 'backward' country, is not quite as freakish as it seems. Throughout the last two hundred years, there has been a widely recognised contrast between the 'modern' aspects of Irish social and political structures — the eighteenth century parliament, the State-sponsored schemes of the nineteenth century, the advanced industrialism of the Belfast region — and the 'antique' aspects of the nation. The contrast was remarkable because the State and the Nation were so entirely at odds with one another. In Yeat's programme for unity of culture, there is a similar blend of the modern Anglo-Irish intellectual tradition and the old Gaelic civilisation. Joyce, in his "Ireland, Island of Saints and Scholars", remarked that

> . . . the Irish nation's insistence on developing its own culture by itself is not so much the demand of a young nation that wants to make good in the European concert as the demand of a very old nation to renew under new forms the glories of a past civilization.[6]

There is, therefore, nothing mysterious about the re-emergence in literature of the contrast which was built into the colonial structure of the country. But to desire, in the present conditions in the North, the final triumph of State over Nation, Nation over State, modernism over backwardness, authenticity over domination, or any other comparable liquidation of the standard oppositions, is to desire the utter defeat of the other community. The acceptance of a particular style of Catholic or Protestant attitudes or behaviour, married to a dream of a final restoration of vitality to a decayed cause or community, is a contribution to the possibility of civil war. It is impossible to do without ideas of a tradition. But it is necessary to disengage from the traditions of the ideas which the literary revival and the accompanying political revolution sponsored so successfully. This is not to say that we should learn to suspect Yeats and respect Joyce. For Yeats, although he did surrender to the appeal of violence, also conceded the tragic destiny this involved. Joyce, although he attempted to free himself from set political positions, did finally create, in *Finnegans Wake,* a characteristically modern way of dealing with heterogeneous and intractable material and experience. The pluralism of his styles and languages, the absorbent nature of his controlling myths and systems, finally gives a certain harmony to varied experience. But, it could be argued, it is the harmony of indifference, one in which everything is a version of something else, where sameness rules over diversity, where contradiction is finally and disquietingly written out. In achieving this in literature, Joyce anticipated the capacity of modern society to integrate almost all antagonistic elements by transforming them into fashions, fads — styles, in short. Yet it is true that in this regard, Joyce is, if you like, our most astonishingly 'modernist'

[6]   *CW* p.157.

author and Yeats is his 'anachronistic' counterpart. The great twins of the Revival play out in posterity the roles assigned to them and to their readers by their inherited history. The weight of that inheritance is considerable. To carry it much further some adjustment must be made. It might be a beginning to reflect further on the tradition of the idea which these two writers embody and on the dangerous applicability it has to the situation in the North.

The danger takes a variety of forms. A literature predicated on an abstract idea of essence — Irishness or Ulsterness — will inevitably degenerate into whimsy and provincialism. Even when the literature itself avoids this limitation, the commentary on it reimposes the limitation again. Much that has been written about Joyce demonstrates this. A recent book, like Hugh Kenner's *A Colder Eye*, exploits the whimsical Irishness of the writers in a particularly inane and offensive manner. The point is not simply that the Irish are different. It is that they are absurdly different because of the disabling, if fascinating, separation between their notion of reality and that of everybody else. T.S. Eliot, in a 1919 review of Yeats, wrote:

> The difference between his world and ours is so complete as to seem almost a physiological variety, different nerves and senses. It is, therefore, allowable to imagine that the difference is not only personal but national.[7]

This sort of manoeuvre has been repeated over and over again in the commentaries on Irish writing and it reappears in commentaries on Irish politics. The Irish, in the political commentary, are seen as eluding what Eliot called a "relation to the comprehensible." This is propaganda disguised as mystification. The sad fact is that the Irish tend to believe it. Yet the variations of adherence (i.e. politically speaking, unionism) and of separation (politically speaking, republicanism) and all the modifications to which they are subject in Irish writing are not whimsical evasions of reality. Our reality has been and is dominated by these variations and their stylistic responses. Although the Irish political crisis is, in many respects, a monotonous one, it has always been deeply engaged in the fortunes of Irish writing at every level, from the production of work to its publication and reception. The oppressiveness of the tradition we inherit has its source in our own readiness to accept the mystique of Irishness as an inalienable feature of our writing and, indeed, of much else in our culture. That mystique is itself an alienating force. To accept it is to become involved in the

---

[7] *The Athenaeum* July 4, 1919, p.552.

spiritual heroics of a Yeats or a Pearse, to believe in the incarnation of the nation in the individual. To reject it is to make a fetish of exile, alienation and dislocation in the manner of Joyce or Beckett. Between these hot and cold rhetorics there is little room for choice. Yet the polarisation they identify is an inescapable and understandable feature of the social and political realities we inhabit. They are by no means extravagant examples of Irish linguistic energy exercised in a world foreign to every onlooker. They inhabit the highly recognisable world of modern colonialism.

Even so, both Joyce and Yeats are troubled by the mystique to an extent that, in contemporary conditions, we cannot afford. The dissolution of that mystique is an urgent necessity if any lasting solution to the North is to be found. One step towards that dissolution would be the revision of our prevailing idea of what it is that constitutes the Irish reality. In literature that could take the form of a definition, in the form of a comprehensive anthology, of what writing in this country has been for the last 300 - 500 years and, through that, an exposure of the fact that the myth of Irishness, the notion of Irish unreality, the notions surrounding Irish eloquence, are all political themes upon which the literature has battened to an extreme degree since the nineteenth century when the idea of national character was invented. The Irish national character apologetically portrayed by the Banims, Griffin, Carleton, Mrs. Hall and a host of others has been received as the verdict passed by history upon the Celtic personality. That stereotyping has caused a long colonial concussion. It is about time we put aside the idea of essence — that hungry Hegelian ghost looking for a stereotype to live in. As Irishness or as Northernness he stimulates the provincial unhappiness we create and fly from, becoming virtuoso metropolitans to the exact degree that we have created an idea of Ireland as provincialism incarnate. These are worn oppositions. They used to be the parentheses in which the Irish destiny was isolated. That is no longer the case. Everything, including our politics and our literature, has to be rewritten — i.e. re-read. That will enable new writing, new politics, unblemished by Irishness, but securely Irish.

Myth and Motherland

by Richard Kearney

Richard Kearney   Born in Cork, 1954. Graduate of University College, Dublin, McGill University, Canada, and the University of Paris. Lectures in philosophy at University College, Dublin.

Founder and co-editor of *The Crane Bag: a Journal of Irish Studies*. Author of *Poetique du Possible* (Beauchesne, Paris, 1984), *Dialogues with Contemporary Continental Thinkers* and *Modern Movements in European Philosophy* (Manchester University Press, 1984). Editor of *The Irish Mind* (Wolfhound Press, Dublin, 1984) and *Heidegger et La Question de Dieu* (Grasset, Paris, 1984).

5

MYTH AND MOTHERLAND

Daniel Berrigan, the American Jesuit, remarked during a visit to Ireland that if you want to understand a society you begin by visiting its prisons and reading its poets. I presume Berrigan was suggesting that it is often in its deviant or dissenting voices that a community expresses those hidden aspirations or alienations which frequently find no place in our more established modes of expression. Berrigan visited Long Kesh prison in Belfast, describing it as the 'bowels of the state', and spoke of a 'kind of hieroglyph being spelt out' by the protesting prisoners: a language of our political unconscious, outlawed by the official discourse. At the other extreme, we have the language of our poets. Poetry also transgresses the legitimised limits of established speech — but in the opposite direction. It does not fall beneath the law, it goes beyond it. Unlike the prisoners', the poets' departure from the norms of discourse is taken as a measure of creation rather than destruction, of liberation rather than incarceration. So that if the prisoners articulate what is considered to be the 'lowest' expression of a society (what Deane, referring to the Maze protest in *Civilians and Barbarians,* called 'the most horrific imagery of degradation'), the poets represent 'the highest' (the most honorific imagery of elevation). Both serve, however, from their opposite poles of dungeon and tower, to subvert the normal edifice of discourse. Both refuse the current consciousness of reality by invoking *something else* which precedes or exceeds it, which remains, as it were, sub-conscious or supra-conscious.

In Ireland, this 'something else' often finds its habitation and its name in *myth*. Thus in our literature, we find a poet like Yeats repudiating the 'filthy modern tide' of contemporary reality in deference to the sacred mythologies of the Celtic Twilight. By means of these mythologies, Yeats hoped to provide a cultural identity transcending the colonial and sectarian divisions which so blighted our national life. In the Maze prison protest we find a similar recourse to mythic idioms — in particular the idiom of sacrificial martyrdom. Resorting to the hunger-strike the prisoners negated their actual political paralysis by realigning their suffering with a mythico-religious tradition of renewal through sacrifice: a tradition stretching back through the 1916 leaders, Terence McSwiney, O'Donovan Rossa and the Fenian Martyrs to the timeless personae of Cuchulain on the one hand and of Christ on the other.

But before analysing in more detail how this collision between myth and reality operates in the discourses of our poets and prisoners, I would first like to establish what exactly is meant by the term 'myth'.

I

Mircea Eliade, a philosopher of comparative religion, states that "myth is thought to express the absolute truth because it narrates a *sacred history*; that is, a trans-human revelation which took place in the holy time of the beginning . . . Myth becomes exemplary and consequently *repeatable*, thus serving as a model and justification for all human actions . . . By *imitating* the exemplary acts of mythic deities and heroes man detaches himself from profane time and magically re-enters the Great Time, the Sacred Time".[1] The mythic appeal to the Sacred Time of the originating heroes of the nation or community is, of course, an appeal to an order outside of historical time (understood as a linear sequence of contingent events). By virtue of their repeatability, the mythic acts of the founding fathers become timeless; they operate according to ritualistic and circular paradigms which redeem us from the depressing facts of the present; they bring history to a standstill and enable us to attend to ancestral voices; they make us contemporaries with the 'dead generations' of the past, transmuting the discontinuities of our empirical existence into the unbroken continuity of an imaginary essence. In short, they create what generally goes by the name of *tradition*.

The mythic attitude might be best summed up as *piety*, or what the Romans called *pietas*: a sense of dutiful allegiance to the claims of father and fatherland. Virgil wrote the *Aeneid* in order to promote the virtues of *pietas* in the Roman state. The *Aeneid* was a fictional rewriting of history, which provided Roman society with a story of foundation, with a narrative of origination dating back to the Homeric myth of the fall of Troy. By thus aligning Latin culture with the foundational legends of Hellenic culture — that is by inventing a continuous link, in the personage of *pius Aeneas*, between the fall of Troy and the rise of Rome — Virgil was able to provide the Emperor Augustus with a sacred prototype which would invest his

[1]   Mircea Eliade, *Myths, Dreams and Mysteries* (Fontana, London, 1968).

present rather shaky rule with an unshakeable, because timeless, authority — a sort of divine right of Emperors. Virgil invented a tradition whose claim to sacred precedent made a nonsense of the secular political disputes which threatened to destroy his society. So that Aeneas is repeatedly described by Virgil as 'pious' not only because he is a quasi-divine hero (begotten of Venus and Anchises) but also and more importantly because he is an agent of ancestral continuity carrying the past into the present (as he bears his father, Anchises, on his back out of burning Troy into the new land of Rome). The message of Virgil's myth is, therefore, one of filial piety towards the father. Just as Aeneas was pious towards his father, Anchises, so too Augustus is pious towards his founding father, Aeneas; and so too Virgil, and by implication the citizens of Rome, are pious towards their father, Augustus. That is what tradition means — *tradere,* carrying or transferring the past into the present and the present into the past. Myths of tradition defy the historical logic of non-contradiction (*either/or*); they lay claim to a supralogical order where something can be *both* what it is *and* what it is not — the past can be present, the human divine, and so on.[2]

✓ The opposite of *piety* is *securality.* If the former pertains to the sacred time of myth, the latter pertains to the profane time of our ordinary experience. The Latin term *saecularis* originally referred to those who lived in the world and were not subject to religious rule. To secularize meant to convert from an attitude of spiritual timelessness to material worldliness. Accordingly, under the rubric of mythic piety might be listed the following properties: unity, eternity, permanence, faith, repetition, ancestry, tradition, essence. Under the rubric of historical secularity we could enter the contrasting values of plurality, temporality, change, reason, innovation, individuality, freedom, arbitrariness and experiment. Or to borrow Lionel Trilling's celebrated distinction, if piety implies a condition of *sincerity* whereby we remain true to the authoritative identity given to us by tradition, then secularity is the condition of *authenticity (auto-hentes:* to fashion for oneself), which sponsors the idea that we are free to create whatever meaning or value we choose: a condition aptly described by Sartre when

---

2   In *The Interpretation of Dreams* (Penguin, New York, 1976), Freud offers a useful comment on the mythic logic of the dream world which ignores the historical laws of causality and contradiction. "In the great majority of cases" he writes, "the causal representation is not represented at all but is lost in the confusion of elements which inevitably occurs in the process of dreaming. The alternative 'either-or' cannot be expressed in the process of dreaming. Both of the alternatives are usually inserted in the text of the dream as though they were equally valid."

he wrote that "we are what we make of ourselves" because "our existence (freedom) precedes our essence (identity)".

Contemporary thinkers have differed on how to assess the claims of myth. Eliade and Jung, for example, defend myth as an inherent dimension of man's religious unconscious. These thinkers justify mythology as a genuine need to rediscover our cultural origins and thus provide ourselves with an indispensable sense of collective rootedness and identity. Whether we like it or not, these thinkers maintain, man is a *homo religiosus;* and this means that "myth itself, as well as the symbols it brings into play, never quite disappear from the present world of the psyche — it only changes and disguises its operations".[3] If we suppress the mythic dimension of our unconscious, abandoning those cultural or religious traditions which provide orthodox, structured expression for our sense of the sacred, myth will not disappear but will find perverse surrogate outlets in our profane experience. Eliade cites the secular cults of fascist or totalitarian leaders as contemporary instances of the perversion of myth. Indeed, the mesmerizing mythology of Big Brother in Orwell's *1984* provides one of the most apt examples of such collective enslavement to a secular abstraction: "The Brotherhood cannot be wiped out because it is not an organization in the ordinary sense. Nothing holds it together except an idea which is indestructible. You will never have anything to sustain you except an idea which is indestructible . . . We are dead . . . We can only spread our knowledge outwards . . . from generation to generation."

But this century has also witnessed the emergence of philosophies opposed to myth in all its guises, sacred or profane. Myth, they argue, is not just a perversion of politics but of religion itself. Emmanuel Levinas makes a sharp distinction between a genuine sense of the 'holy' (*Saint*) which opens human nature to a transcendent, monotheistic deity and the mythic category of the 'sacred' (*Sacré*) which confines us to polytheistic idolatry and primitivism. Rudolph Bultmann calls for a radical 'demythologisation' of belief which will disengage the Judeo-Christian Revelation from the magico-mystery rites and apocalyptic Saviour cults of pagan origin. "To understand Jesus' fate as the basis for a mythic cult," he writes, "and to understand such a cult as the celebration which sacramentally brings the celebrant into such fellowship with the cult-divinity that the latter's fate avail for the former as if it were his own — that is a Hellenic mystery idea" (*The Theology of the New Testament*). To demythologise religion means therefore to

---

[3]   Mircea Eliade, *Myths, Dreams and Mysteries* (Fontana, London, 1968).

demystify those mystic accretions of the Judeo-Christian heritage which derived from Hellenic, Orphic or Celtic paganism. Another theologian, Jürgen Moltmann, extends this demythologising program into a critique of the sacrificial cult of martyrdom.[4]

The common feature of these various efforts to 'demythologise' western culture is the sponsoring of a *logos* of rational critique against a *mythos* of irrational mystification which is considered subversive not only of individual liberty but of our humanistic civilization as a whole.

II

How does this theoretical dispute between mythic piety and secular reason relate to our prisoners and poets? Let's begin with some concrete examples of the prison discourse. A conspicuous, if somewhat cliché-ridden feature of the H-Block campaign was the use of the mythic rhetoric of sacrificial martyrdom. The aura of cliché does not however in the least diminish the emotive and evocative power of this rhetoric. In fact it adds to it. For repetition, as we noted, is essential to the *efficacity* of myth. But precisely because it become a prereflective password of the tribe, myth often escapes critical analysis.

The IRA's ideology of martyrdom inverts what goes by the name of normal logic (at a parliamentary or military level), and subscribes to a mythic logic which claims that defeat is victory, past is present, etc. This mythic logic is not, as commonly assumed, some irrational reflex action (and therefore undeserving of analysis); it is a highly structured and strategic method of combining contraries which secular reason

---

4   See for example the following passage from Moltmann's *The Theology of Hope* (SCM Press, England, 1967): "The influence of cultic piety shows itself not only as a formal event in the self-preservation of Christianity on Hellenistic soil, but quite certainly extends also to the understanding of the event of Christ. The Christ event is here understood as an epiphany of the eternal (past) in the form of a dying and rising *Kyrios* of the *cultus* . . . Initiation into the death and resurrection of Christ then means that the goal of redemption is already determined, for in this baptism eternity is sacramentally present . . . the Cross becomes a timeless sacrament of martyrdom which perfects the martyr and unites him with the heavenly Christ". Moltmann rejects this cult of sacrifice as a perversion of true christianity. More recently, the French thinker, René Girard, has gone as far as to repudiate all forms of myth on the grounds that they presuppose a sacrificial scapegoat upon whom the evils of a divided society are predicated. The blood sacrifice of the scapegoat is considered a means of purifying society and of restoring it to a new order of harmony and unity. And through this purificatory sacrifice, observes Girard, the reviled scapegoat often becomes a deified mythic hero (*Le Bouc Emissaire*, Grasset, Paris, 1982).

keeps rigidly apart.[5] The IRA's ideology is *sacrificial* to the degree that it invokes, explicitly or otherwise, a 'sacred' tradition of death and renewal which provides justification for present acts of suffering by realigning them with recurring paradigms of the past and thus affording these acts a certain timeless and redemptive quality. By insisting that their current campaign 'is not ten years old but over sixty years old',[6] the IRA are identifying with the Republican tradition of the 1916 and Fenian leaders. So that while, on the one hand, the Provos present themselves as a highly modernised, unsentimental and pragmatic paramilitary movement, they confess, on the other, to taking their "inspiration and experience from the past . . . from the native Irish tradition" founded on "our Irish and Christian values".[7]

Taking this reference to tradition as our cue, we find obvious precedents for the sacrificial myth of martyrdom in the discourse of the 'past' generations of Republicans: Pearse's funeral oration at O'Donovan Rossa's grave in 1915; the reply by the volunteers in 1916 to the British call to surrender, that they "had gone there to die not to win"; the victory achieved by the rebels not when they shot *at* the British from the General Post Office but when they were shot *by* the British in Kilmainham jail; and the celebrated maxim of Terence McSwiney, the Sinn Féin Lord Mayor of Cork who died on hunger strike in 1920: "It is not those who can inflict the most, but those who suffer the most who will conquer". All of these confirm the appeal to and the appeal of sacrifice.

The present IRA are not unmindful of the power of this sacrificial tradition and have commemoratively exploited it to secure widespread sympathy (*sym-pathein*; to suffer with) for

---

5   As Lévi-Strauss remarked in *Structural Anthropology* (Penguin, 1968), myth operates according to a different kind of logic, a logic of unconscious symbolism, which is quite as rigorous as scientific logic. In *Tristes Tropiques* (Atheneum, New York, 1971), Lévi-Strauss describes this mythic logic as "the fantasy production of a society seeking passionately to give symbolic expression to the institutions it *might* have had in reality" had the socio-political conditions of that society been more conducive to the solution of its problems. But since "on the social level, the remedy was lacking", the society finds itself impotent to realize its desired goals and so begins "to dream them, to project them into the imaginary". In short, for Lévi-Strauss, myth can serve as an ideological strategy with the purpose of inventing symbolic 'solutions' to problems which remain irresolvable at the socio-political level.

6   Statement by IRA Army Council spokesman talking to Ed Moloney in *Magill* (September, 1978).

7   Statement by provisional Sinn Féin in *Where Sinn Féin Stands*, (Kevin St., Dublin, January, 1970).

their prison campaigns. While it is true that the IRA are hard-nosed, feet-on-the-ground militants who would like nothing better that to achieve decisive military victory over the British Army, it is equally true that once faced with imprisonment, by which successful military action is rendered impossible, they make no bones about subscribing to McSwiney's view that those who suffer the most will ultimately be vindicated.

The IRA have not short memories. We find William McKee, a noted Belfast Republican, declaring that 'the war will be won in the prisons'. In 1980, a Maze prisoner reiterated this sentiment when he wrote on the wall of his cell: "I am one of many who die for my country . . . if death is the only way I am prepared to die". The *many* here refers to a long litany of martyrs whose sacrificial death for Ireland has been translated into the 'sacred debt' of the 'freedom struggle'. One of the most popular responses to this sacrificial attitude has been the emergence of ballads, snatches or rhymes which, like myths, are often authored by nobody yet known to everybody.

The extraordinary propaganda power of mythic logic has not been lost on the IRA leadership. There is impressive evidence to show that support for the 'cause' increases in reaction to sacrificial suffering more than to military aggression, more through hunger-strikes than bomb-strikes. Quite apart from christening the murder of 14 Derry civilians by the British Army in 1972 as 'Bloody Sunday' (the same term attributed to the massacre of innocent civilians in Croke Park by the British Army in 1920), Sinn Féin did not hesitate to present the recent H-Block campaign in the mythic idioms of martyrdom. In so doing, they succeeded in providing their movement with a broad base of support in the Catholic nationalist community, North and South.

Just as Pearse identified his death with the sacrifice of Christ in the poem *A Mother Speaks,* written on the eve of his execution, so too the death of the hunger-strikers in Long Kesh was frequently presented in sacrificial terms. Posters showed battered, tortured or starved prisoners in Christ-like posture, the wire of Long Kesh transformed into a crown of thorns, the H-Block blanket into a crucifixion cloth. So that while it is clear that the military wing of the movement increasingly use the no-nonsense secular idioms of Marxist-Internationalism (e.g. the liberation of the oppressed working class from capitalist exploit-ation and imperialist aggression), the 'prison wing' of the move-ment often invoke the more mythic idioms of Gaelic, Catholic tribalism. Daily mass in Long Kesh became, by the prisoners' own admission, a major source of sustenance by enabling them to identify with the 'Gethsemane' agonies of Pearse and other Fenian martyrs.[8] And Fathers Murray and Faul introduced their H-Block document of Christmas 1979 with a drawing of the Pope blessing the kneeling prisoners and quoted the Pontiff's Drogheda statement of the same year that 'the Law of God stands in judgment over all reasons of state'. Gaelic classes also became a regular feature of life in Long Kesh. And one could hardly find a more apt description of the psychological and ideological force of this recourse to the language of the tribe than in Cardinal O' Fiach's statement after his visit to the prisoners in July, 1978: "In the circumstances I was surprised that the morale of the prisoners was high. From talking to them it is evident that they intend to continue their protest indefinitely and it seems they prefer death rather than submit to being classed as criminals. Anyone with the least knowledge of Irish history knows how deeply rooted this attitude is in our country's past. In isolation and perpetual boredom they main-tain their sanity by studying Irish. It was an indication of the triumph of the human spirit over adverse material surround-ings to notice Irish words, phrases and songs being shouted from cell to cell and then written on each cell wall with the remnants of toothpaste tubes". The prisoners' hieroglyph mentioned by Berrigan is here deciphered by the Cardinal.[9]

As is now obvious, the impact of the prison protest was not confined to the prison. Sands, Carron and Adams were elected to Westminster less because they represented a quasi-Marxist guerrilla movement of liberation than because they articulated a tribal voice of martyrdom, deeply embedded in the Gaelic, Catholic Nationalist tradition. This is surely why Adams, for example, was so embarrassed by Republican offensives (partic-ularly if they involved civilian casualties) during his election campaign. Which is not to deny that there is double-think at work in both elected and electorate. But it is precisely because of this double-mindedness, that it is simplistic to declare that a vote for Sinn Féin is always a vote for violence. Unless, that is, one means a vote for violence 'suffered' rather than violence 'inflicted'. That the IRA themselves subsequently interpret this vote as an endorsement of their military offensive is undeniable. But that does not diminish the initial ambivalence in the mind of the voter.

---

8   Tim Pat Coogan, *On the Blanket*, (Ward River Press, Dublin, 1980).
9   For a more detailed discussion of this and other statements on the mythology of sacrificial martyrdom in Irish Republicanism see my *Myth and Terror* in *The Crane Bag*, Vol 2, Nos 1 and 2, Dublin, 1977; The *IRA's Strategy of Failure* in *The Crane Bag*, Vol 4, No 2, Dublin 1980; and *Terrorisme et Sacrifice: las cas de l'Irlande du Nord* in *Esprit*, Paris, April, 1979.

The key word here is ambivalence. The prison campaign showed that the Republican movement operates in terms of two distinguishable, if not always distinct, discourses. On the one hand, there is a rhetoric that leans towards the Gaelic Catholic Nationalist idioms of myth, tradition, piety and martyrdom. On the other hand, there is the secular discourse of military action, political electioneering and social work; and it is here that we find the new Sinn Féin vocabulary of class struggle, advice centres and liberal pluralism (e.g. their 'progressive' attitude to matters of sexual morality such as divorce, contraception or the recent Amendment debate on abortion).

But a similar tension between mythic and anti-mythic discourse can also be witnessed in the broader spectrum of Irish politics. In the Unionist camp (represented in the Northern Assembly) one might cite the opposition between the 'tribal' Ian Paisley and the more 'liberal' Robert McCartney. In the Forum of constitutional nationalism, one found differences emerging between the Haughey-Mallon wing and the Fitzgerald-Hume-Spring wing.[10] Indeed, this tension between the idioms of *piety* and *secularity* has a number of historical precedents in Irish politics. It goes back as far as the old debate between the Fenian or 1916 leaders who advocated a form of militant nationalism and such proponents of parliamentary nationalism as O'Connell, Parnell and Redmond. And it surfaced again in the now classic alternatives represented by De Valera's 'traditional' Ireland and Lemass's 'modern' Ireland. To talk in terms of such oppositions is, of course, to simplify — several of the political figures mentioned frequently straddled the divide — but it does exemplify in however stark a form, a basic polarisation between a *mythologising* form of politics which interprets the present in terms of a unifying past (sacred tradition) and a *demythologising* form of politics which interprets the present in terms of a pluralising future (secular progress).

III

In our literature we also discern two opposing tendencies. One led by Yeats sponsored mythology. The other, including Beckett, Flann O'Brien and Joyce, resolved to demythologise the pretentions of the Revival in the name of a thoroughgoing

---

10 Contrast, for example, Haughey's opening address to the Forum where he argued for the revival and retention of "our most fundamental aspirations" with Hume's opening address where he declared that the Forum is not a "nationalist revival mission" and that one of the reasons for our failure to resolve the national problem up to this may have been due to our inability to place the creation of a New Ireland "above some of our most cherished assumptions."

modernism; it endeavoured to liberate literature from parochial preoccupations with identity into the universal concern of language as an endlessly self-creative process. As Beckett put it, language ceased to be *about* something and became *that something itself*.

Yeats offered the myth of Mother Ireland as spiritual or symbolic compensation for the colonial calamities of historical reality. The mythological Mother would restore the lost national identity by calling her sons to the sacred rite of blood-sacrifice whereby they would re-enter the sacred time which transcends historical time — and thus undo the wrongs of history. In short, since reality told a story of division and dispossession, Yeats replied with answering symbols of unity and self-possession.

At the religious level, Yeats sought in myth an idealised Celtic paganism *pre-existing* the colonial rupture of Ireland into the sectarian denominations of Protestant and Papist. This prehistorical religion of the pious Celt would, Yeats argued in *The Trembling of the Veil* (1922), provide the segregated Irish people with a common currency of 'Holy Symbols' — eternal archetypes first given 'by God to the bright hearts of those long dead' and transcending the sectarian quarrels of the present. Accordingly, Yeats affirmed that a mythic religion — founded in the Collective Unconscious or *Anima Mundi* of the race — would recollect the fragmented communities and individuals of the land in the form of a 'memory beyond all individual memories': a memory which is not deliberately chosen by us but 'comes into the mind from beyond the mind'. The true vocation of Irish poets, he had declared in 1898, is to form a 'company of Irish mystics' whose 'religious philosophy' will transform both poet and non-poet into 'ecstatics and visionaries'. Thus we find Yeats openly confessing to the Fenian leader, John O' Leary, that 'the mystical life is the centre of all that I think and all that I write' — presuming, no doubt, to have hit upon a visionary mythology shared by poet and politician alike.

At the literary level, Yeats was convinced that the religious *Unity of Spirit* could be translated into a corresponding *Unity of Image* which would enable us to see 'all life as a mythological system' and thereby serve as the 'originating symbol of a national literature' (*Trembling of The Veil*). Yeats was deeply disappointed by the fact that the Anglo-Irish Literary Revival inaugurated by himself, Synge and Lady Gregory had been spurned by the Catholic middleclasses, the Gaelic Leaguers and many of the Republican nationalists. Pearse, for example, in a letter to *An Claidheamh Soluis* in 1899, had declared that

"If we once admit the Irish-literature-is-English idea, then the language movement is a mistake . . . Against Mr. Yeats personally we have nothing to object. He is a mere English poet of the third or fourth rank and as such he is harmless. But when he attempts to run an 'Irish' Literary Theatre it is time for him to be crushed". Yeats' recourse to the legendary images of Celtic mythology may thus be interpreted as an attempt to make peace between the opposing interests of class, creed and language. It was a plea for a cultural *continuity* based on a homogenous Ancient Irish Sect which *preceded* all contemporary disputes. In its way, it was a plea for Tone's ideal of a common Irish tradition embracing 'Protestant, Catholic and Dissenter'.

Finally, at a political level, we find Yeats contriving to transmute the violent conflicts of the National Struggle into the salvific myth of a 'terrible beauty'. In his poem, *Easter 1916*, Yeats admits that those rebel leaders whom he had previously dismissed in a 'mocking tale or gibe' have been 'transformed utterly' by the mythic rite of blood-sacrifice. The motley crew of disparate individuals have been transmuted into a visionary sect — 'Hearts with one purpose alone'. They have, in short, been redeemed from the contingencies of history and become magically contemporaneous with the mythic personages of the Great Time of the Holy Beginning. Thus Pearse, for example, is transposed into the archetypal figure of Cuchulain. "When Pearse summoned Cuchulain to his side", asks Yeats in *The Statues*, "What stalked through the Post Office?" The quarrel between Pearse and Yeats *in life* is thus resolved *in myth*: they find common cause outside of time. By means of the ritualistic repetition of blood-sacrifice, Pearse ceases to be an historical individual opposed to Yeats for reasons of class, creed and language, and becomes one with the timeless tradition of 'Dead generations', including Anglo-Norman, Dane, Celt and so on — a tradition in which Yeats and the Anglo-Irish community could also share. (This is surely why Yeats can endorse Pearse's sacrificial myth of an 'enduring nation': "For Padraig Pearse has said/That in every generation/Must Ireland's blood be shed".)

* * * * * *

But modern Irish writers were not all of one mind. Beckett, for example, repudiated Yeats' mythologising as sanctimonious clap-trap. Beckett revelled in discontinuity and alienation. He abhorred the mythic idioms of collective continuity and community, declaring his major concern to be the exploration of the 'rupture of the lines of communication'. Not only did he dismiss the notion of shared 'Holy Symbols' but he rejected the very idea of symbolism as an illusory attempt to create correspondences between the private anguish of the author and some external system of universal values. 'No symbols where none intended', he retorted to those critics who sought to translate his record of misery into myth. 'There can be no communication', he bluntly insisted, 'because there is nothing to communicate'.

Not surprisingly, therefore, Beckett had nothing but contempt for the myth-making of the Irish Literary Revival which he dismissed, in an essay on 'Recent Irish Poetry' (1936) as the 'altitudinous complacency of the Victorian Gael'. In opposition to such 'antiquarian' writers as Yeats, Clarke and Corkery who endeavoured to 'flee from self-awareness' by resurrecting the lost traditions of some 'hidden Ireland', Beckett promoted a counter-tradition of Irish authors who embraced a modernist Continental literature of self-reflection. In this latter category he included Coffey, Devlin, McGreevy and, by implication, himself. What Beckett admired in these authors was the admission that they belonged 'nowhere' — their refusal to drop through the escape-hatch of myth whereby the 'self is either most happily obliterated or else so improved and enlarged as to be mistaken for the decor'. Like Beckett, these writers began with their own nothingness and wrote about the impossibility of ever translating this nothingness into something else. Theirs was an art of 'pure interrogation'. Question without answer. The very idea of a National Literature was a nonsense for Beckett — a myth in the worst sense of the word. He commended O'Casey's anti-nationalism in *Juno and the Paycock* and interpreted this send-up of our tribal mythologies (particularly of blood-sacrifice) as a testimony to the collapse of all notions of national identity: "mind and world come asunder in irreparable dissociation — *chassis*". But Beckett's most sustained attempt to demythologise the pretensions of the Irish cultural Revival is recorded in his first novel, *Murphy*. Here Beckett parodies the literary nationalism of authors like Yeats and Clarke in the personage of Austin Ticklepenny, a 'pot poet' who felt it his 'duty to Erin to compose' verses 'bulging with as many minor beauties from the Gaelic prosodoturfy as could be sucked out of a mug of Beamish's porter'. Talk about Ancient Irish Sects offered no solace for Beckett. The Filthy Modern Tide had dissolved all mythic and national securities; it had to be confronted head on by each solitary self. This is why Beckett emigrated to Paris and resolved to stay on there in the forties preferring, as he put it, France at war to Ireland at peace.

Joyce too revolts against the use of myth to sacrifice the creative individual to tribal cults. By demythologising the fetishized myths of the motherland, he hoped to emancipate the self from the constraints of the past. To this extent, he shared not only Beckett's preference for exile but also his abhorrence of insular nationalism, which he derided as a 'pale afterthought of Europe'. But Joyce differed from Beckett in that he was not content to simply abandon myth for modernism, swopping Dublin for Paris or his own language for a foreign one (French). After several months in exile, Joyce wrote that he did not wish only to 'Europeanise Ireland' but also to 'Hibernicise Europe'. He wanted to blend a fidelity to his local origins with a counter-fidelity to the more anonymous culture of the Continent. He wanted, as it were, Ireland to become more universal and Europe to become more particular. To this end, Joyce did not hesitate to have recourse to myth — albeit myth in a new sense.

In *Ulysses,* Joyce uses one kind of myth to demythologise another. Molly, for example, is the antithesis to the 'Mothers of Memory' which Stephen identifies with the paralysing 'nightmare of history'. Her passionate affair with Blazes Boylan contrasts with the self-sacrificing Virgin of *Mother-Church*; she hasn't a word of the *Mother-Tongue*; and she commemorates the sensual Andalusian maidens of Gibraltar rather than the Celtic Goddesses of the *Mother-Land* such as Róisín or Caithlín. Yet Molly is both mother and memory — as the final soliloquy testifies. And as such she does achieve the proportions of a mythic figure whose double commitment to the particularity of everyday experience *and* to the universality of European mythology (she is identified with Penelope in line with the Greek myth of Ulysses) enables her to demythologise the stereotypes of our tribal myths. As Joyce explained in a letter to Valéry Larbaud: "Penelope has the last word". By playing mythic archetypes off against mythic stereotypes in this way, Joyce was suggesting that we can be liberated from our pre-established narratives of identity without capitulating to the modernist cult of solitary individualism. What Joyce found attractive about the Greek mythology of Ulysses (Bloom) / Penelope (Molly) / Telemachus (Stephen) was its *foreignness* — its ability to offer us alternative models of universality whose very otherness to our native models would enable us to redefine our experience in a new way, in a way untrammelled by the restrictive pieties of the motherland. Accordingly Molly is for Joyce a distinctively *Irish* woman precisely because she has been freed from those clichés of Irish womanhood which would have prevented her expressing herself as she *really is*. And yet by identifying her with the open-ended mythic model of Penelope, Joyce is allowing this Irishwoman to be Everywoman. In short, Joyce seems to be saying that myth is good when it opens the familiar to the foreign and is bad when it reduces the foreign to the familiar.

Of course, this in no way reflects a bias against Irish mythology *per se* in favour of Greek mythology. If Joyce was a Greek writer he might well have chosen Caitlín ní Houlihán as his liberating model! Moreover, in *Finnegans Wake*, Anna Livia Plurabelle represents a universal mother figure drawn from both non-Celtic and Celtic mythologies (Anna was the ancient Celtic Goddess and Livia derives from Liffey). In this respect, Joyce is brushing Irish myths against the grain enabling them to coalesce with alien myths. He is, as it were, deconstructing his tradition from within by exposing it to heterogenous traditions from without. *Finnegans Wake* teaches us that Dublin is 'Doublin' — itself and not itself. It teaches us that our sense of tradition is not some pre-ordained continuity which makes us all the same. Myth is revealed as history and history as myth. Joyce thus shows that our narrative of cultural self-identity is itself a fiction — an 'epical forged cheque' — and that each one of us has the freedom to re-invent our past. Accordingly, myth need not be the suspension of the individual, as Yeats and Beckett believed. For myth can only survive in and through the multiple re-inventions of different individuals and these individuals can best communicate through the universalising idioms of myth. This is why Joyce presents Anna Livia Plurabelle as a model of *unity in plurality*, a 'bringer of plurabilities' who is 'every person, place and thing in the chaosmos of alle . . . moving and changing every part of the time'.

IV

A common idiom which emerges from our analysis of the prison discourse of martyrdom and the poetic discourse of tradition, is the myth of motherland. I have treated the political and literary discourses separately, but they frequently overlap. The writings of Pearse represent a good example of this. In the name of a national Revival, Pearse sought a return to the foundational myths of our identity, to a sense of rootedness in the past which would allow us to make the break with the 'alien' culture of colonial Britain which had uprooted and alienated us from our original sense of ourselves. These foundational myths, which would enable the orphaned child to return to the security of its maternal origins, were identified by Pearse in a positive sense with the three mothers of our historical memory: the mother church of the Catholic revival; the motherland of the nationalist revival; and the mother-tongue of the Gaelic revival. In the opening and closing sentences of the Easter Proclamation of 1916, for example, we find an implicit conflation of these revival idioms. Opening with a ceremonial Gaelic address to *Poblacht na hEireann*, the text operates, in certain key phrases, a rhetorical correlation between i) the Catholic symbolism of a mystical reunion with dead martyrs through the sacrifice of the Mass and ii) the mythological Gaelic idea of Mother Ireland calling on her sons to shed their blood so that the nation might be restored after centuries of historical persecution.

Elsewhere Pearse is more explicit in his conjugation of the Catholic and mythological idioms of martyrs sacrificing themselves for the sake of the Eternal Mother. In his farewell poem from his death cell in Kilmainham, he identifies his own martyrdom with that of Christ who also 'had gone forth to die for men'. The poem is appropriately entitled *A Mother Speaks* and ends with the poet comparing his own mother's faith in his powers of sacrificial renewal with Mary's faith in the resurrection of the crucified Christ — "Dear Mary, I have shared thy sorrow and soon shall share thy Joy". And in Pearse's play, *The Singer*, we find the hero McDara identifying his sacrificial resistance to the impious foreign enemy with Christ's redemptive suffering at the hands of the Romans: "I will stand up before the Gaul as Christ hung naked before men on a tree". Nor did Pearse have any difficulty in sliding from the martyred Christ to the martyred Cuchulain as a means of translating the defeats of historical time into the victory of mythological timelessness.

It is within this mythic context of sons sacrificing themselves for the motherland that we must understand Pearse's enigmatic claim that 'bloodshed is a cleansing and a sanctifying thing' and that 'life springs from death'. But it was perhaps Thomas MacDonagh, another 1916 leader, who best summed up the sacrificial motif when, in his *Literature in Ireland*, he described the recurring aspiration for national renewal as the 'supreme song of victory on the dying lips of martyrs'. Not surprisingly, Yeats enthusiastically embraced this idea.

These sentiments were by no means confined to Pearse and the poets. They epitomised the overall *mythos* of the 1916 Rising which gained common currency in the popular imagination — particularly after the signatories were executed. Posters appeared on the streets of Dublin showing the martyred Pearse reclining *pieta*-like on the bosom of a seraphic celestial woman brandishing a tricolour: a mixture of Mother Ireland, the Virgin Mother of Christ and the Angel of the Resurrection.

Is it possible that such mythic idealisations of Irish woman-hood might be somehow related to the social stereotypes of the Irish woman as pure virgin or equally pure son-obsessed mother? In the historical evolution of our religious ideology we witness a shift away from the early Irish church which was quite liberal in sexual matters and assigned an important role to woman, to a more puritanical religion which idealised woman as an other-worldly creature of sublime innocence. And it is perhaps no accident that this shift coincided in some measure with the colonisation of Ireland. The more dispossessed the people became in reality the more they sought to repossess a sense of identity in the realm of ideality. Since the women of colonized Ireland had become, in James Connolly's words, the 'slaves of slaves', they were, in a sociological sense at least, obvious candidates for compensatory elevation in the realm of myth and mystery? The cult of female virginity surely contributed to this sublimating process of purification. Woman became as sexually intangible as the ideal of national independence became politically intangible. Both entered the unreality of myth. They became aspirations rather than actualities. Thus it might be argued that a sociological transposition of Irish women into desexualised and quasi-divine mothers corresponds somehow to an ideological transposition of Ireland from a Fatherland (the term *an t-athardha* was used to denote Ireland in much bardic poetry up to the 17th century) into idioms connoting a Motherland. As psychoanalysis reminds us, the mother has always been a powerful unconscious symbol for one's forfeited or forbidden origins.

This idealised myth of Irish womanhood was reinforced in the late nineteenth century by a certain counter-reformational leaning in Irish Catholicism towards a cult of the Virgin Mother (mariolatry) witnessed in the rise of confraternity and abstin-ence movements which championed the virtues of self-sacrifice and sexual purity. Indeed it is interesting how elements in the Irish Hierarchy — which offered women little or no power in ecclesiastical reality — increasingly came to identify Ireland as a virginal Motherland which could best be served by safeguard-ing our native purity of 'faith and morals' against the evil influence of alien cultures.[11] To betray these ideals of national purity was, as Bishop Harty of Cashel remarked early in the century, to 'bring shame on the Motherland'. The more colon-ially oppressed the Irish became in historical reality the more

---

[11] I have tried to develop this theme further in a study entitled 'Faith and Fatherland' in *Ireland: Dependence and Independence — The RTE/UCD lectures* (*The Crane Bag*, Dublin, 1984).

spiritualized became the mythic ideal of the Motherland. One need only compare the redemptive Mother Eire of 1916 — the decently-clad Caitlín who preferred her sacrificial sons and lovers dead than alive — with the barebreasted carnal maiden of the French Revolution's *République*. In short, Caitlín was less a living creature of the worldly present than a mythic memory of an other-worldly past.

But the most important overall factor in the development of our myths of motherland remains, arguably, the political colonization of Ireland. After the plantations of the 17th century, Ireland became more frequently identified with a vulnerable virgin ravished by the aggressive masculine invader from England: the *Sasannach*. In the *Aisling* poems of the 18th century the suppressed or 'hidden' Ireland was personified as a visionary daughter or *spéirbhean* threatened by the alien *Sasannach*. (Or inversely, following the same logic, as a shameless hag — *meirdreach* — who lifted her skirts for the invader's pleasure).[12] In the nineteenth and twentieth centuries, the passive daughter seems to assume the more militant guise of a mother goddess summoning her faithful sons to rise up against the infidel invader so that through the sacrificial shedding of their blood, she might be miraculously redeemed from colonial violation and become free and pure again — that is, restored to her pristine virginity of language, land and liturgy. Is it conceivable that the evolution of our myths of nationhood narrates some sort of transition from fatherland (*athardha*) to daughterland (*aisling*) and to motherland (*Caitlín na hEireann*), which obliquely mirrors the history of our political unconscious? If such an hypothesis were tenable — a matter for the scholars to decide — it could suggest that the indentification of 'colonized' Ireland as

---

12 These poems, as Daniel Corkery remarked, are more racial than personal in character; they are typical of mythic forms of expression in that they subordinate individual utterance to the archetypes of national experience. Ancestral heroines and heroes are more important than actual privacies of feeling. Thus, for example, we find a *spalpín* poet like Owen O'Rathaille revering Ireland as a 'fair daughter of celestial powers' (do geineadh ar gheineamhain/di-se an tír uachtaraigh), and declaring that he will suffer 'amid a ruffian hoarde' until the ancient heroes return from over the sea of death (go bhfuillid na leoghain tar tuinn). This poetic cult of the *spéirbhean* was not confined to the Gaelic poets; it also became a common feature of such Fenian Anglo-Irish poets as Mangan, Ferguson or Darcy Magee who cultivated the *aisling* motif as a means of translating colonial history back into pre-colonial myth — to that Great Time of the Holy Beginning when, as Magee wrote in his poem *The Celts*, 'beyond the misty space/of twice a thousand years/in Erin old there dwelt a mighty race.' For a vivid fictional treatment of these themes, see Ronan Sheehan's title story in his *Boy with an Injured Eye* (Brandon, 1983).

celestial daughter or mother, represents a symbolic projection of a *prohibited* sense of self-possession. Dispossessed of a present, might not our poets have sought their national identity in idealized 'female' personifications of a pre-colonial past or post-colonial future?

V

Hitherto I have been approaching myth at the level of description rather than prescription. I have been trying to analyse how it works, rather than asking how it should or should not work — the ethical question.

Keats once remarked that imagination is amoral and apolitical, transcending all considerations of good and evil. 'The poetical character', he wrote, has no ethical commitments and takes 'as much delight in conceiving an Iago as an Imogen'. 'What shocks the virtuous philosopher', he concluded, 'delights the chameleon Poet'. Keats was no doubt right — up to a point. And that point, I suggest, is often signalled when literary myth spills over into political myth. So that while a poet may be exempt from moral intentions — we all prefer poetry without propaganda — he or she can never be wholly exempt from moral consequences. Yeats tried to draw an indivisible line separating 'perfection of the work' from 'perfection of the life'. But this dualism is too convenient; and it is ultimately untenable. Whatever about the moral rights and wrongs of his support for militant Republicanism, Yeats' literary cult of mythic heroes also led him to espouse, however provisionally, the fascist rhetoric of Eoin O'Duffy at home and of Mussolini abroad. And this aberration found voice in some of his worst verse — e.g., 'What's equality? Muck in the yard'. Similarly Francis Stuart, another exponent of the immunity of literary myth from moral judgment, turned to fascism, as his pro-Nazi broadcasts from Berlin during the war and his novelistic apologia for this action after the war — *Black List Section H* — testify.

There can be no poetic licence for political barbarism. *Mythos* can never be insulated from the ethical critique of *Logos*. The Greeks knew this and tried to combine both by laying the foundation for our western civilisation in the complementary partnership of poetics and philosophy. To remove either of these foundation stones from the edifice of our culture is to collapse into prejudice, to sponsor an apartheid of *civilians* versus *barbarians*. The poets and prisoners are there to remind us that myth often harbours memories or expectations which established reason has ignored at its peril — and at the peril of the society it claims to safeguard. But by the same token, myth must never divorce itself from rational and ethical self-critique to such an extent that it sacrifices humanity to the fanaticism of a lifeless abstraction. Yeats was right, I submit, when he wrote that 'too long a sacrifice can make a stone of the heart'; he was wrong when he recommended that Imagination be 'brought to that pitch where it casts out/ All that is not itself'. Imagination and reason, *mythos* and *logos,* are the indispensible Siamese-twins of the mind. Their surgical separation can only result in the death of both. Thomas Mann realised this when he wrote in the wake of the Nazi nightmare: 'If *mind* is the principle, the power, which desires the good; if it is sensitive alertness towards the changing aspects of truth, a 'divine solicitude' which seeks to approach what is right and requisite at a given time, then it is political, whether or not this epithet sounds pretty. It seems to me that nowadays nothing alive escapes politics. Refusal is politics too; it is a political act on the side of the evil cause'. Mann seems to be recommending that we put an end to the uncritical excommunication of art from politics and of politics from art. The politician and the artist must reconvene a debate in common pursuit of the good.

Myth is a two way street. It can lead to perversion (bigotry, racism, anti-semitism, fascism, totalitarianism); or it can lead to the projection of genuine utopias whereby individuals, communities and indeed the community of nations as a whole, can identify with the goal of *universal* liberation. If we need to demythologize, we also need to remythologize. It is our ethical duty therefore to use our powers of *logos* to discriminate between the authentic and inauthentic uses to which *mythos* is put in our culture. For if myth is often a response to repression, it can become repressive in its own right. We cannot afford to dispense with the difficult task of determining when myth emancipates and when it incarcerates, that is, when it evolves into a creative symbol and when it degenerates into a mere idol. And this is not as simple as uncritically assuming that our established division between poets (as an instance of emanci- pation) and prisoners (as an instance of incarceration) has done the job for us. There are prisoners behind bars who should not be there and some poets who should be there. What is at issue here is much more complex than the black and white categories of the *status quo*. What is required is a radical interrogation of those mythic sedimentations from our *past* and those mythic aspirations for our *future* which challenge our *present* sense of ourselves, which disclose other possibilities of being. And this interrogation ultimately rests upon the ethical necessity to distinguish between myth as an *open-ended process* which frees us from the strait-jacket of a fixed identity; and myth as a *closed product* which draws a magic circle around this identity excluding dialogue with all that is other than ourselves.[13]

Without mythology, our hopes and memories are homeless; we capitulate to the mindless conformism of fact. But if revered for its own abstract sake, if totally divorced from the challenge of reality, mythology becomes another kind of conformism, another kind of death. We must never cease to keep our mythological images in dialogue with history; because once we do we fossilise. That is why we will go on telling stories, inventing and re-inventing myths, until we have brought history home to itself.

---

[13] See my dialogue with the French philosopher Paul Ricoeur on this question, entitled *Myth as the bearer of possible worlds* in *The Crane Bag*, Vol 2, Nos 1 and 2, Dublin, 1978.

Anglo-Irish Attitudes

by Declan Kiberd

Declan Kiberd Lectures in English at University College, Dublin. Current director of the Yeats Summer School. A graduate of Trinity College, Dublin, where he later lectured in Irish, he has also taught at the University of Kent at Canterbury, after postgraduate study at Oxford University.

Has written extensively, both in Irish and English, on the literature and politics of modern Ireland. Publications include *Synge and the Irish Language* (London, 1979) and *Men and Feminism in Modern Literature* (London, 1985).

Has lectured on Irish writing in America, Canada, Japan, France, Italy, Spain, Portugal and Switzerland, and is currently preparing a book entitled *Revival or Revolution?: Modern Irish Writing and the Socialist Tradition.* Presenter of a weekly arts programme on Irish television.

6

ANGLO-IRISH ATTITUDES

'Every power in nature must evolve its opposite in order to realise itself', wrote Giordano Bruno, 'and opposition brings reunion'. What is true of nature may also be true of nations. The English did not invade Ireland — rather, they seized a neighbouring island and invented the idea of Ireland. The notion 'Ireland' is largely a fiction created by the rulers of England in response to specific needs at a precise moment in British history. The English have always presented themselves to the world as a cold, refined and urbane race, so it suited them to see the Irish as hot-headed, rude and garrulous — the perfect foil to set off British virtues.[1] The corollary of this is also true. The Irish notion of 'England' is a fiction created and inhabited by the Irish for their own pragmatic purposes. Coming from an almost neolithic community on wind-swept seashores, the Irish immigrants in British cities had no understanding of life in the anonymous workplaces into which they were plunged. They found it easier to don the mask of the garrulous Paddy than to reshape a complex urban identity of their own. As early as 1818, John Keats described the Irish as cunning blusterers and gallous fellows who were 'sensible of the Character they hold in England and act accordingly to Englishmen'.[2] Within their tightly-knit communities, these immigrants continued to subscribe to their ancient pieties, while happily conforming to the folk image of the stage Irishman in affairs of business and politics. Acting the buffoon, they seemed harmless and lovable adults to those Englishmen who might otherwise have resented their competition for jobs in a contracting work-force. An art of fawning duplicity was perfected by the most successful Irish businessmen, who acted the buffoon while making shrewd deals which outsmarted their English rivals.

---

[1] See Declan Kiberd, 'The Fall of the Stage Irishman', *The Genres of the Irish Literary Revival*, ed. R. Schleifer (Dublin, 1980), 39-60. Some of these opening points recapitulate the main thesis of that essay.

[2] John Keats, *Letters of John Keats*, selected by Frederick Page (Oxford University Press, London, 1954), 149.

For almost two centuries, both the Irish and the English have been using each other's territory as a gigantic laboratory in which to conduct experiments which would be unthinkable in the domestic context.[3] In recent years, for example, thousands of Irish girls have travelled to London, Manchester and Birmingham in order to procure the abortions which are still illegal in their native land. In the same period, crowds in Belfast and Derry have been fired on by a British Army employing those plastic bullets which the Home Secretary still prohibits from use on domestic rioters in such trouble-spots as Southall and Toxteth. Lest these seem depressing examples, it should be added that the manifestations of the 'laboratory theory' can be positive and encouraging. Because Ireland was a testing-ground for the new educational theories of the 1830s, her people had the benefits of efficient, nationalised schools long before their counterparts in Britain itself. Equally, it has often been argued that the cultural life of England has been immensely enriched by many Irish writers, artists, actors and teachers who have chosen that country as the prime location for what Yeats once called 'an experiment in living'. The entire tradition of Anglo-Irish comedy seems to be based on the conviction that each country is an experimental laboratory, to be used at will by the neighbouring people. George Bernard Shaw once described Ireland as an open-air sanatorium to which all Englishmen should be sent for a time in order to learn flexibility of mind. But the attitude is reciprocal. Yeats said that to an Irishman England is fairyland.

'Was there ever an Irish man of genius who did not get himself turned into an Englishman as fast as he could?' asked Henry Craik in an immortal line of an otherwise unremarkable letter. No better illustration could be found than the career of Oscar Wilde, which began with his arrival as a student in the Oxford of 1874. There he began to dedicate himself to the noble art of the pose. According to Yeats, Wilde in England 'perpetually performed a play which was in all things the opposite of all that he had known in childhood and youth. He never put off completely his wonder at opening his eyes every morning on his own beautiful house and in remembering that he had dined yesterday with a Duchess'. The home which Wilde had abandoned in Dublin was, on the other hand, 'dirty,

---

[3] For historical applications of the 'laboratory theory', see Patrick O'Farrell, *Ireland's English Question* (New York, 1971) and *England and Ireland since 1800* (Oxford, 1975); Joseph Lee, *The Modernisation of Irish Society* 1848-1918 (Dublin, 1973); and Oliver MacDonagh, *Ireland: The Union and Its Aftermath* (London, 1973).

untidy and daring' and it was presided over by two eccentric parents who seemed to Yeats to have stepped straight out of a bad stage-Irish melodrama. Sir William Wilde, although a most eminent surgeon and scholar, was reputed to be the dirtiest man in Dublin, 'beyond soap and water', reported Shaw, 'as his Nietzschean son was beyond good and evil'. Sir William's studies of the antiquities and archaeology of Ireland were matched by Lady Wilde's collections of folklore, her militant feminism and her outpourings of nationalist verse. To her second son she bequeathed a love of the theatrical and a conviction of the rights of women to work and to political activity. 'Why should there be one law for men and another for women?' asks Jack in *The Importance of Being Earnest*, a play which is a satire on the manic Victorian urge to antithesis. Wilde's is an art of inversion where each side exemplifies qualities which we would normally expect in its opposite, as every dichotomy dichotomises. The traditional contrast in the comedy of manners between corrupt city slickers and unfallen rural characters is exposed as a gross simplification. Jack and Algy's cynicism is seen to be a mere front for an unquenchable openness to new experience, while the apparent innocence of the country Canon Chasuble is seen to conceal a more sinister kind of knowingness. This inversion of the expectations of the audience may also be found in the play's depiction of sexuality. So it is the women who read heavy works of German philosophy and attend university courses, while the men lounge elegantly on sofas. The men are filled with romantic impetuosity and breathless surges of emotion, but it is the women who cynically discuss the finer points of the male physique. When Algy proposes to Cecily, it is *she* who runs her fingers through his hair and asks if it curls naturally. (Yes — with a little help from others). Lord Bracknell, for his part, knows that a man's place is in the home, for, in the words of his niece, 'once a man begins to neglect his domestic duties he becomes painfully effeminate, does he not? And I don't like that. It makes men so very attractive'. In all these scenes Wilde is applying his doctrine of the androgyny of the healthy personality. This would find immortal expression in the wisecrack that "All women become like their mothers. That is their tragedy. No man does. That's his'. The apparent sexism of the first half of the jibe is fully exploded by the sharp feminist intelligence of the conclusion.

Antithesis was the master-key to the entire Victorian cast of mind, causing people to make absolute divisions not just between English and Irish, but also between men and women, good and evil, and so on. Wilde saw that by this mechanism the English male could attribute to the Irish all those traits of

85

poetry, emotion and soft charm which a stern Victorian code had forced him to deny in himself; but he knew from experience that the two peoples are a lot more alike than they care to admit — that the Irish can as often be cold, polite and calculating as the English can be sentimental, emotional and violent. In the same fashion, Wilde saw Victorian men demand that their women epitomise those virtues of softness, domesticity and fidelity which a harsh business ethic had led them to suppress in themselves. In *The Importance of Being Earnest* Wilde showed that such an antithesis quite simply does not work. As often as not, it is the women in that play who are businesslike in making cynical economic calculations about a proposed marriage, while the men remain steadfastly impractical. Far from being an exponent of the witty paradox, Wilde is interested in the moment of modernism when the ancient antithesis dissolves to reveal an underlying unity. Like Yeats, he could see that talent perceives differences, but only genius discerns unity.

This same inversion of conventional expectations would explain the pose adopted by Wilde in England. All the norms of his childhood were now to be reversed. His father had been laughed at by society, so he would mock society first. His father had been an unkempt, fluent Irishman so he would be a fastidious, urbane Englishman. From his mother he had inherited a gigantic and ungainly body, which recalled all too painfully the gorilla-like form of the stage Irishman in Tenniel's cartoons. To disarm such racialist critics, the young dandy concealed his massive frame with costly clothes and studied the art of elegant deportment. The ease with which Wilde effected the transition from stage Irishman to stage Englishman was his ultimate comment on the hollowness of the antithesis, on the emptiness of both notions.

In rejecting this manic urge to antithesis, Wilde satirised the determinism of Victorians as diverse as Marx and Carlyle, who believed that upbringing and social conditioning determined consciousness. The belief that the Irishman was the prisoner of heredity, diet and climate,[4] like the conviction that woman is by nature docile, subservient and deferential, were twin attributes of Victorian determinism. This determinism is taken to its *reductio ad absurdum* in Wilde's account of two girls each of whom accepts that it is her ineluctable destiny to

---

4   For a full account of Anglo-Saxonist theory, see L. Perry Curtis Jnr., *Anglo-Saxons and Celts: A Study of anti-Irish Prejudice in Victorian England* (Connecticut, 1968); and also his *Apes and Angels: The Irishman in Victorian Caricature* (London, 1971).

love a man named Ernest.[5] The very plot of the play is an example of a determinism so extreme as to render the concept idiotic and banal. Its machinery creaks with an over-obviousness which is clearly designed to subvert the convention of the well-made play by carrying it to an outrageous degree. Algy predicts that the girls will only call each other sister after they have called one another other names as well; and, sure enough, within ten minutes, Cecily and Gwendolen are embarked on a vicious quarrel, as life imitates art with grim predictability. The girls, precisely because they seem to have been more exposed to Victorian education than the men, show a touching faith in determinism. Ever since Cecily had heard of her wicked uncle, she could think of nothing else. But it is not a belief in determinism which prompts Algy to play along with her charade of fictional letters and engagements between them. Rather, he expresses deep admiration for the fertile imagination of a girl who had the courage to reject the tedious all-female regime of Miss Prism and reincarnate some of the missing male elements in the Ernest who is a pure concoction of her mind. Like the androgynous Wilde, she rejects the notion of an antithesis between herself and others, because she has already recognised the existence of that antithesis in herself. In doing so, she also rejects that other great fiction of the Victorians, the black-and-white distinction between good and evil. Just before meeting her wicked uncle she says: 'I have never met any really wicked person before. I feel rather frightened. I am so afraid he will look just like everybody else'. Wilde is one of the first modernist writers to take for subject not the knowledge of good and evil, but what Lionel Trilling was later to call the knowledge of good-and-evil. He insists that men and women know themselves in all their aspects and that they cease to suppress those attributes which they may find painful or unflattering.

Yet the Victorian Englishman continued to attribute to the Irish all those emotions and impulses which his strict code had led him to deny in himself. Thus, if John Bull was industrious and reliable, Paddy was held to be indolent and contrary; if the former was mature and rational, the latter must be unstable and emotional; if the Englishman was adult and manly, the Irishman must be childish and feminine. So the Irish joined hands with those two other persecuted groups, women and children; and at the root of many an Englishman's suspicion of the Irish was an unease at the woman or child who lurked within himself. The implications of this equation have

---

5   On this, see Christopher Nassaar, *Into the Demon Universe* (Yale University Press, 1974), 135-6.

been spelled out by Perry Curtis — either as woman or as child, the Irishman was incapable of self-government. The flaunted effeminacy of Wilde, no less than his espousal of the inner world of the child in his stories, may well be a sly comment on these hidden fears. All of his essays on Ireland question the assumption that just because the British are industrious and rational the Irish must be lazy and illogical. The man who believed that a truth in art is that whose opposite is also true was quick to point out that every good man has an element of the woman in him, just as every sensitive Irishman must have a secret Englishman within himself — and *vice-versa*. With his sharp intelligence, Wilde saw that the image of the stage Irishman tells us far more about English fears than Irish realities, just as the still-vibrant Irish joke tells us far less about the Irishman's foolishness than about the Englishman's persistent and poignant desire to say something funny. In his case, Wilde opted to say that something funny for the English, in a lifelong performance of Englishness which constituted a parody of the very notion. By becoming more English than the English themselves, Wilde was able to invert, and ultimately to challenge, all the time-honoured myths about Ireland.

George Bernard Shaw was another writer who treated England as a laboratory in which he could define what it meant to be an Irishman. In his play *John Bull's Other Island,* the defrocked priest Peter Keegan found wonders in Oxford that he had never seen in Ireland, but on his return home he discovered that the wonders had been there all the time. 'I did not know what my own house was like', he concludes, 'because I had never been outside it'. In similar fashion, the mock-villain Broadbent only discovers what it means to be an Englishman when he pays a visit to Ireland. 'Ireland', wrote Shaw, 'is the only spot on earth which still produces the ideal Englishman of history'. *John Bull's Other Island* is Shaw's attempt to show how the peoples of the two islands spend most of their time acting an approved part before their neighbour's eyes and these assigned parts are seen as impositions by the other side rather than opportunities for true self-expression. In the play stereotypes are exploded, for it is the Englishman Tom Broadbent who is a romantic duffer, while the Irishman Larry Doyle is a cynical realist. The underlying reasoning is sound, for the Irish have become fact-facers through harsh poverty, while the English have enjoyed a scale of wealth so great that it allows them to indulge their victims with expansively sentimental gestures.

On the one hand, Broadbent cynically plots the ruin of the village of Roscullen and packs a gun before his visit to the place; on the other hand, he fills his head with sentimental stage-Irish claptrap about the charm of rural Ireland. As his cynical Irish partner observes, he keeps these separate ideas in watertight compartments, with 'all the compartments warranted impervious to anything it doesn't suit you to understand'. So Broadbent is charmed by the antics of Tim Haffigan, a Stage Irishman who wishes him the top-o-the-mornin', until Doyle exposes him as a fraud and an impostor, born not in Ireland but in the streets of Glasgow. Doyle insists that the Stage Irishman is a creation of the British folk mind: 'all Haffigan has to do is to sit there and drink your whiskey while you humbug yourself', he warns Broadbent, but to no avail, for the English partner attributes this anger to 'the melancholy of the Celtic race'. Doyle remarks that sweeping generalisations about the Celtic race constitute the most insidiously aggressive ploy of all the tactics used by imperialistic Englishmen. Such talk does more harm than ten coercion acts, because it gives rise to the feeling, bitterly and wittily mocked by Seamus Deane, that 'if the Celts stay quaint they will also stay put'.[6]

As an empirical fact-facing Irishman, Larry Doyle felt uneasy in his own country — his youthful desire was to learn how to do something and then to get out of Ireland in order to have the chance to do it. The play itself seems to suggest that an Irishman will succeed far better in England than in Ireland, where the only successful men are all English. In Ireland, Broadbent plays the role of amateur of the Celts, the English liberal in search of round towers and fresh-faced colleens. So Broadbent, by his outrageous antics in the role of English duffer, manages to see only the Ireland he has come to see, a land of buffoons, derisive laughter and Celtic whimsy, where a pig can be taken for a ride in his car and an Englishman voted the fittest man to represent Roscullen in Parliament. Broadbent adopts the protective coloration of the stage-English buffoon, to the enormous entertainment of the natives, who reciprocate by adopting the protective coloration of the stage-Irish peasant, taking tea at the wrong time of the day and laughing hysterically at every event which ensues. Larry Doyle foresees that, for his antics, Broadbent will not be laughed out of town but will be rewarded with Larry's girl and Larry's seat in Westminster: 'He'll never know they're laughing at him — and while they're laughing he'll win the seat'.

The driver who ferried Broadbent into Roscullen told him that the finest hotel in Ireland was there, but there is no hotel

---

6   Seamus Deane, 'Irish Poetry and Irish Nationalism', *Two Decades of Irish Writing: A Critical Survey*, ed. D. Dunn (Cheadle, 1975), 8.

— just seventeen pubs. Aunt Jude excuses the driver: 'sure he'd say whatever was the least trouble to himself and the pleasantest to you'. This is the psychology which underlies the acting of all parties, both Irish and English. On the Irish side, Patsy Farrell, the callow labourer, exudes an air of helpless silliness which, says Shaw, 'is not his real character, but a cunning developed by his constant dread of a hostile dominance, which he habitually tries to disarm by pretending to be a much greater fool than he really is. Englishmen think him half-witted, which is exactly what he wants them to think'. This, however, is precisely the strategy adopted already by the conquering Englishman, for, according to Larry Doyle, 'the Englishman does what the caterpillar does. He instinctively makes himself look like a fool, and eats up all the real fools at his ease while his enemies let him alone and laugh at him for being a fool like the rest. Oh, nature is cunning, cunning'. In other words, at root the English and Irish are identical peoples, who have nevertheless decided to perform extreme versions of Englishness and Irishness to one another in the attempt to wrest a material advantage from the unsuspecting audience of each perform-ance. Each group projects onto the other all those attributes which it has denied in itself, but at bottom both peoples are alike. This socialist perception is embodied in Hodson, the servant of Broadbent, who does indeed find in Ireland the flexibility of mind to disown his master and to point to the common cause of the dispossessed Irish labourer and the exploited English proletariat.

Shaw's play, like Wilde's career, is a radical critique of the Anglo-Irish antithesis so beloved of the Victorians and, it must be stressed, of that last Victorian, W.B. Yeats. By the simple expedient of presenting a romantic Englishman and an empirical Irishman *John Bull's Other Island* mocks the ancient stereotype. Of course, that is not the end of the story, for, by his performance of absurd sentimentality, Broadbent effectively takes over the entire village on the terms most favourable to himself, while Larry Doyle loses his cynical self-composure in the face of the ruin of his people. Larry's sophisticated intellect paralyses him into inactivity, for he has grown too subtle and too cynical, foolish in his very cleverness, whereas Broadbent's blinkered version is finally what allows him to be so efficient, so clever in his very foolishness. In the end, the Anglo-Irish antithesis is questioned, but only to be reasserted in a slightly modified form.[7] It is left to the prophetic Peter Keegan to

---

[7] On this, see Alfred Turco Jnr., *Shaw's Moral Vision: The Self and Salvation* (Cornell University Press, Ithaca and London, 1976), 178.

explain Broadbent's efficient victory: 'let not the right side of
your brain know what the left side doeth. I learnt at Oxford
that this is the secret of the Englishman's power of making the
best of both worlds'. By mastering the stereotype, by pretending
to be a stage-fool, Broadbent has eaten up all the real fools,
just as Larry predicted. Ireland has on this occasion been a
useful laboratory for another English experiment.

It is no accident that the British Prime Minister Balfour
should have attended Shaw's play with cabinet colleagues on
four separate occasions, or that King Edward VII should have
broken his chair with laughing at the production. After all, the
play gratified English vanity, by managing at once to criticise
the old stereotype and at the same time suggesting that it was
true in a deeper and subtler way. English audiences not only
found their ancient prejudices confirmed by a witty Irish playwright, but could leave the theatre with unexpected and
sophisticated evidence in support of their ancient bias. It was
all too fitting that Shaw should have described himself as a
faithful servant of the British people. There is a real sense in
which his own play is itself an artistic casualty of the vice of
compartmentalisation which he satirises. The plot issues in an
emphatic victory for the efficient and romantic Englishman,
but all the subversive witticisms have been uttered by a cynical
but ineffectual Irishman. This was the very same dualism which
Shaw detected in the comedies of Wilde, each of which contains
some scathing witticisms at the expense of the institutions of
British class society, but whose power to disturb is wholly
disarmed by the reassuringly conventional nature of Wilde's
plots. In such plots, the aristocratic society always wins out, as
in *The Importance of Being Earnest,* where Lady Bracknell can
marry off her Gwendolen to a young man of her own exalted
class. Both Wilde and Shaw are finally English writers in the
strict terms of Shaw's own definition of Englishness as a talent
for keeping ideas separate in watertight compartments. The
right side of the dramatist's brain never knows what the left
doeth, and the plots of their plays are entirely at variance with
the subversive one-liners and jokes. All of which is a measure of
the artistic constraints on any socialist dramatist who sought a
career in the London of the time.

Yeats's solution to this dilemma was to gather a native
Irish audience and create a native Irish theatre in Dublin — to
express Ireland to herself rather than exploit her for the
foreigner. He accepted the Anglo-Irish antithesis, but only on
condition that he was allowed to reinterpret it in a more flatter-
ing light. Whereas the English had called the Irish backward,
superstitious and uncivilised, the Gaelic revivalists created an

idealised counter-image which saw her as pastoral, mystical, admirably primitive. Yet such a counter-image was false, if only because it elevated a single aspect of Ireland into a type of the whole. 'Connaught for me is Ireland', said Yeats; but Ireland is not Connaught — rather she is a patchwork quilt of cultures, as she was before the Normans invaded. George Watson has devoted a valuable section of *Irish Identity and the Literary Revival* to an elaboration of this point, showing how the folklorism of Yeats confirmed the traditional image of the Irish as subservient and menial[8] — only now they were deemed menial in colourful and interesting new ways. 'The cracked looking-glass of a servant' was how Joyce's hero Stephen described such an art. It is an apt image, not just of Yeats's hopeless rehabilitation of the modes of deference but also of Joyce's own escape into modernism, for what a cracked looking-glass really shows is not a single but a multiple self.

Subsequent writers came increasingly to question the legacy of Yeats and to turn instead for guidance to that socialist tradition of Irish writing initiated by Wilde and Shaw. Both Sean O'Casey and Brendan Behan record in their auto-biographies the shock of recognition on reading *John Bull's Other Island*. In *The Plough and the Stars* O'Casey goes to great lengths to imply that the English and Irish have a great deal more in common than they care to admit. He drops his final curtain on the spectacle of British soldiers sipping tea that had been brewed for their Irish enemies and embarking on that same fragile attempt at domesticity with which the tenement-dweller Nora Clitheroe began the play. Even the clichés employed by both sides in the conflict turn out to be inter-changeable. When the British gun-boat pounds the inner city, Fluther Good complains 'that's not playing the game', the precise phrase used by a British soldier when he discovers that the rebels are firing dum-dum bullets.[9] (In fact, no report on the Rising offered evidence to convict the rebels of this charge, but O'Casey is more anxious to complete his Anglo-Irish parallelism than to give a clear account of the facts).[10] When a passing British soldier is asked what he is doing in Dublin, he says 'defending my country'. He receives the swift retort: 'You're not fighting for your country here, are you?' Clearly, the

---

[8] George Watson, *Irish Identity and the Literary Revival* (Croom Helm, London, 1979), 121.

[9] See B.L. Smith, *O'Casey's Satiric Vision* (Kent State University Press, 1978), 48, on this parallelism.

[10] C. Desmond Greaves, *Sean O'Casey: Politics and Art* (Lawrence and Wishart, London, 1979), 121.

imperialist nature of the British presence in Ireland was not something that O'Casey wished to deny, but it is given a tragic irony by the soldier's baffled avowal 'I'm a socialist myself'. Socialists on both sides have been sucked into the maelstrom of nationalism; and even the radical Covey begins to make glowing references to 'General' Pearse, whom he has unwittingly promoted in the ranks.

Some decades later, in Brendan Behan's *The Hostage,* the response of a British soldier to Irish cross-questioning is emphatic: 'You can take me out of it as soon as you like. I never bloody well asked to be brought here'. Asked why the British are still in Ireland, he replies equally enough: 'And what about the Irish in London? Thousands of them. Nobody's doing anything to them'. As a lowly hostage, he knows that the Secretary of State in London will hardly weep into his whiskey over the loss of a single private. His captor Pat turns out to be the soldier's secret double. One is used by the IRA, the other by the British Army; but both know that the struggle in which they are mere pawns is obsolete in an age of hydrogen bombs. In his depiction of the kilted piper Monsewer, Behan clinches the point. The cockney hostage exclaims when first he sees the old Republican: 'Just like our old Colonel back at the depot. Same face, same voice. Gorblimey, I reckon it is him'. Behan is covertly repeating Patrick Kavanagh's suggestion that the so-called Irish Revival, like the actual Irish repression, is a plot by disaffected public-schoolboys.

In all of the plays discussed, opposites turn out to be doubles; clichés employed at the start by one side are appropriated by the other; and each time an Irishman meets an Englishman, he simply encounters an alternative version of himself. The Irish Question is really the English Question, and *vice-versa.* The Irish are accused of never forgetting, but that is because the English never remember. The Irish are accused of endlessly repeating their past, but they are forced to do so precisely because the English have failed to learn from theirs. In his recent book *States of Mind,* the historian Oliver MacDonagh has shown just how many features of the current crisis are re-runs of an earlier historical reel. In a heady closing chapter entitled 'England's Opportunism, Ireland's Difficulty', he shows how the British authorities have contrived to repeat the same old mistakes. For example, the failure of London to ameliorate Catholic grievances and to promote power-sharing between Catholics and Protestants in the years immediately following the Act of Union not only explains the grim harvest of the 1820s and 1830s, but may also sound a warning-note for those who failed to maintain the executive set up in the 1970s

93

after Sunningdale. Similarly, the recall of Fitzwilliam and the repression of 1795 seem to MacDonagh to constitute the same script as that enacted with the institution of internment in August 1971, and to the same effect. Epoch-making events like the Union of 1801 or the proroguing of Stormont in 1972 arose, says MacDonagh, from 'an absorption in the immediate'. 'Each stroke was seen in terms of a current problem, in terms of breaking an impasse, of cutting a hopeless tangle'.[11] The use of the word 'stroke' will amuse students of Irish politics in the 1980s, reminding them that attempts to wrestle immediate advantages from short-term manoeuvres in the field of Anglo-Irish relations are not the sole preserve of London politicians. But it is certainly true that the surrender of Merlyn Rees to the bullyboys of the Ulster Workers' Council — a surrender made in direct contravention of the advice offered by Len Murray and the TUC — was the prelude to the current drift of British policy back to its customary aimlessness. The slow political death of Gerry Fitt began with that surrender, and Gerry Adams was simply the man who hammered a final nail into a coffin prepared for Fitt by Merlyn Rees. This also explains the extraordinary sentimentalisation of Gerry Fitt by English liberals and labour-leftists, for he is an eloquent reminder to them of their own guilt and spinelessness when put to the test in 1974. Since then, there has been no British policy at all. 'From being serious but never desperate', concludes MacDonagh, 'the Ulster question had, apparently, been reclassified in London as desperate, but never serious'.[12]

These just observations destroy some hoary Anglo-Irish clichés, but only after preceding chapters of *States of Mind* have resuscitated some others. MacDonagh sees the English view of history as developmental — they take short views in the conviction that all things ripen in the fullness of time. The Irish he depicts as an ahistorical people who reject notions of chronology, see history as the endless repetition of familiar themes with no hope of resolution, and pay scant heed to the squatters' rights conferred by the centuries on the invading English. The English he sees as empiricists who judge each case with due regard to the situation ethics of time, place and property. The Irish are taken to be a nation of moral absolutists whose longer memories invoke the superior rights inherent in law and morals. For them history is never really history unless it exactly repeats itself, dramatising their longstanding moral

---

11 Oliver MacDonagh, *States of Mind: A Study of Anglo-Irish Conflict* 1780-1980 (Allen and Unwin, London, 1983), 142.

12 Ibid., 143.

claim in each generation. MacDonagh adds such polish to the familiar cliché that the Irish are prisoners of their own past. But his final chapter explodes this opening thesis by proving that it is the English who force such dreary repetitions on the Irish.

MacDonagh might have been nearer the truth had he suggested that it is the English who are obsessed with their past, while the Irish are futurologists of necessity. Certainly, an eavesdropper on Thatcher's England and Fitzgerald's Ireland could not think otherwise. In one country, ancient dwellings and Viking sites are lovingly preserved; in the other, they are cursorily destroyed. As British power and prestige decline, English leaders turn more and more to the past for comfort and consolation — Thatcher rededicates herself to the values of Victorians, Steel and Owen rediscover ninteenth-century liberalism, and Benn looks to the early Chartists. And while all this is going on, the Irish appoint a Forum to debate their own future. Like all colonised peoples whose history is a nightmare, the Irish have no choice but to live in the foreglow of a golden future. For them history is a form of science fiction, by which their scribes must rediscover in the endlessly malleable past whatever it is they are hoping for in an ideal future. So Connolly and Davitt could pretend to find in the Gaelic past their ideal system of communal landholding; so de Valera and Hyde could claim to have resuscitated a pastoral idyll and a vibrant traditionalism; so Synge and O'Casey could mask their calls for sexual liberation with references to the liberalism of Merriman and the Brehon laws; and so Conor Cruise O'Brien, dreaming of a denationalised and peaceful land, can rediscover such a place in the Ireland which failed to rise in any numbers in 1916. In such a land, the word 'history', like the word 'Gaelic', means whatever you want it to mean, and therefore means nothing.

Dr. O'Brien's contribution to the rewriting of history has one great value. It has exploded the myth of the bellicose Paddy and demonstrated that the besetting Irish condition is not pugnacity but paralysis, not idealism but pragmatism, not passion but cunning. Curiously, this was also the diagnosis offered by J.M. Synge in *The Playboy of the Western World*, which proved that those Irish who warmed to a 'gallous story' (or song or ballad) would not necessarily applaud an actual 'dirty deed', unless that deed had occurred elsewhere, on the far side of a patrolled border, or in the past. Almost sixty years before O'Brien, Synge had shocked his countrymen by revealing to them the ambiguity in their attitude to violence. Synge saw that the heroic myth of Cuchulain, perpetuated by Yeats and

Pearse, was an attempt to gratify the self-esteem of Irishmen at home, but that it did this only at the expense of feeding the ancient lie about the 'fighting Irish' abroad. Joyce also often spoke against the common misconception of the Irish as quarrelsome, asserting that they were on the contrary gentle and passive like the Jews. Although today the Irish still retain the reputation for aggression, there is even less basis than ever to the myth. Ireland has been occupied by foreign armies since 1169, but it now almost two hundred years since anything like an open mass army of Irishmen resisted the forces of occupation. In the same period the English have fought literally dozens of wars, and will in the future doubtless fight many more. And yet there are still millions of English people who think that the Irish are bellicose. This major discrepancy between English and Irish attitudes to violence is best illustrated by the events which followed the Easter Rising. The story of 1916 is not so much the story of the Rising as of the Executions. To the British authorities, the handful of rebel leaders were mere traitors, not greatly different from the dozens of soldiers in the trenches of Europe who deserted or defected every week. Their fate was that of the traitor, and, as such, would scarcely have merited a paragraph on an inside page of a newspaper. But the Irish people, passive and peaceable to a fault, had no stomach for such reprisals, and they were appalled by the protracted orgy of official violence in Dublin. The key to the rise of Sinn Féin in subsequent years lies not in an Irish love of violence but in a principled recoil from it. Insofar as Sinn Féin became publicly implicated in bloody deeds, its reputation suffered reversals. Only the English could have come up with forces like the Black-and-Tans or the B-Specials to copperfasten support for the rebels. As George Bernard Shaw wearily observed: 'The notion that Ireland is the only country in the world not worth shedding a drop of blood for is not a Protestant one, and certainly not countenanced by English practice'.[13]

Shaw's contributions to the Anglo-Irish debate caused one Dublin workman named Pat O'Reilly to raise subscriptions for a patriotic plaque on the house of his birth. 'Your inscription is a blazing lie', wrote Shaw, 'all my political services have been given to the British Labour movement and to international socialism'.[14] As an internationalist, Shaw had mocked 'that

---

13 George Bernard Shaw, Preface to *John Bull's Other Island* (Bodley Head, London, 1971), 831.

14 Michael Holroyd, 'GBS and Ireland', *Sewanee Review*, Vol. LXXXIV, No. 1, (Winter 1976), 52.

hollowest of fictions',[15] the notion of an *English* or an *Irish*
man. To that limited extent, Shaw seemed to become a fellow-
traveller with those High Tories at the far end of the political
spectrum who would claim that West Belfast is no different
from East Finchley. The socialist dream was also the imperialist
pretence — that the whole world could be recast in a single
image — and it was this imperial pretence which caused a
Gaelic poet to fear the imminent emergence of West Britain,
'Saxa Nua darb ainm Éire'. Victorian schoolchildren opened
their day with an invocation at morning assembly:

> I thank the goodness and the grace
> That on my birth has smiled,
> And made me in these Christian days
> A happy English child.

Yet the streets through which those children walked home from
school exploded such a theory — streets filled with soldiers,
laws based on emergency legislation, houses harbouring
fugitives, all testified that Ireland was in some way different.

Faced with these realities, the British intelligentsia of the
nineteenth century came up with its notion of an antithesis
between all things English and Irish. For some, this expressed
their revulsion at the spectacle of the neighbouring barbarians.
For others, Ireland seemed to embody valuable qualities such
as pastoral beauty, emotional spontaneity and spiritual idealism
which had slowly disappeared from the British way of life.
British literary figures began to find in Ireland all those traits
which they feared they were losing in themselves. Inevitably,
there was much that was sentimental, and even patronising, in
their view. They gave the Irish a reputation for colourful speech
which did not always square with the facts, a reputation so
powerful that it still clings to those Irish writers who have done
most to repudiate it. The 'scrupulous meanness' of the opening
paragraphs of *Dubliners*; the attack on 'poetry talk' as a
substitute for action in the plays of Synge; the attempt by
Kavanagh to write a poetry that flirts with the possibility of
becoming prose; the success of Beckett's translation to French,
a language in which it is 'plus facile d'écrire sans style' — all
betoken a critique of Irish wit and wordplay. Joyce turns his
suspecting glance onto the English liberal Haines, his phrase-
book at the ready for those wisecracks and witticisms that
refuse to come; Kavanagh repents of the paddy-whackery of
The Green Fool with a lifetime of linguistic self-denial; Beckett
is so ashamed of his early versions of 'Sodom and Begorrah' that

---

[15] G.B. Shaw, Preface to *John Bull's Other Island*, 814.

he changes language rather than risk repeating the mistake. Even Yeats, aware of his own fatal propensity for eloquence, resolved to take rhetoric and wring its neck, and if he did not always succeed, then at least he pointed the way. A poem like 'Easter 1916' is a highly ironic catalogue of cliché, done with only part of the tongue in the cheek. By the time Flann O'Brien emerges with his resuscitated banalities, the tongue will be wholly lodged in the side of the mouth. The Irish revival, seen in this light, may be less an explosion of verbal colour, than a dignified assertion of a people's right to be colourless. To give this thesis the extended consideration it deserves would be to risk dismantling one of the most potent myths in the history of Anglo-American criticism of Irish writing.[16]

Confronted with a set of clichés which compound insult ('violent') and patronisation ('eloquent') in equal measure, it is not surprising that Irish writers and critics often bite the liberal English hand that feeds them. But the sole alternative is to be told by the High Tories that West Belfast is like East Finchley. For better or worse, the audience of British liberals and leftists remains Ireland's most firm hope. (The notion that the Tories will initiate the final withdrawal, just as the Republicans and not the Democrats extricated America from Vietnam, is probably wishful thinking). Irish writers, political and literary, have for more than a hundred years addressed themselves to that modest but influential constituency, often with painful results for both sides. Those Englishmen who take an interest in Irish affairs often feel that rejection and contempt are their only thanks. Their interest often seems incomprehensibly quixotic to their fellow-countrymen who know just how often Ireland has been the graveyard of English political hopes. These English students of the Irish situation see themselves as conscience-stricken idealists, reaching across the divide of centuries, only to be accused by a new generation of Irishmen of repressive tolerance, of being the subtlest exploiters of all, of being the reincarnation of Broadbent and Haines. It was in such a mood that Donald Davie wrote 'Ireland of the Bombers'. It was, doubtless, in such a mood that Robert Kee read many of the Irish responses to his *Ireland: A Television History*. Here, he must have felt, was a decent English liberal, scrupulously telling both sides of the tragic story in a helpful and level-headed way. Here, many Irish felt, was another liberal posing as a moderate and factual Englishman between warring Irish extremists — and thereby perpetuating the greatest single

---

[16] For further comments on this, see S. Deane, 'Heroic Styles: The Tradition of an Idea', Field Day Pamphlet No. 4 (Derry, 1984).

illusion that underlies the British presence in Ireland. Mr. Kee's series did immense good in Ireland as well as in England. There can hardly have been a single citizen who did not learn something new, and often uncomfortable, about his own past. But the more skilled it was in demolishing all the minor myths, the more successful it became in renovating the greatest myth of all. In marked contrast, the ITV series entitled *The Troubles* employed no 'impartial' British front-man and resorted to a flat, descriptive script read in clipped, impersonal tones by a hired actress. It was considerably more radical in its interpretation of events than the BBC Series, and, of course, no less 'loaded' or prejudged. But it had the merit of allowing the Irish realities to speak for themselves.

What all this demonstrates is simple enough — the power of an ancient myth to reappear in a new guise even when men think that it has been exploded forever. The well-intentioned Englishman who thinks that he might be part of the solution turns out to be part of the problem; and the dispassionate Irishman who sets out to question British clichés often finds himself forced covertly to appeal to them, if only to initiate a dialogue. Those who refuse this compromise are thrown out of court; those who accept the constraints are often forced to betray the cause they love. The forces which neutralised the subversive paradoxes of Wilde and Shaw are no less potent in the 1980s than they were in the 1880s. The attempts to explain Ireland to the English are scarcely more advanced. Just as the English took the traditionalist Yeats to their hearts and shunned the modernist Joyce, so now they shower praise and prizes on those analysts of the Irish imbroglio who offer culture rather than cash by way of explanation.

The reception accorded to the late F.S.L. Lyons's Ford Lectures at Oxford University in 1978 is a case in point. These were published in the following year by the Clarendon Press under the title *Culture and Anarchy in Ireland: 1890-1939*. Professor Lyons's thesis was that 'the essence of the Irish situation is the collision of a variety of cultures, Gaelic, English, Anglo-Irish and Ulster Protestant'. He argued that no political solution will be successful unless it is based on an understanding of the intricacies of this interlocking pattern. In seeking to provide the historical basis for such an understanding, he was at pains to reject the more fashionable Marxist analysis of men like Michael Farrell and Eamonn McCann:

> The ancient quarrel is, of course, about power (wrote Lyons), and about its economic base, as well as about its economic manifestations. But such clichés can hardly

satisfy us. If we ask further what are the ends for which the possession of power is coveted, we may perhaps come closer to the truth about Ulster. In that small and beautiful region different cultures have collided, because each has a view of life which it deems to be threatened by its opponents; and power is the means by which a particular view of life can be maintained against all rivals. These views of life are founded upon religion, because this is a region where religion is still considered as a vital determinant of everything important in the human condition.[17]

Professor Lyons demonstrated that sectarian rioting began in 1813, long before Catholics were numerous enough in cities to constitute an economic threat to the employment of Protestants. Furthermore, he documented with rare descriptive power that curious blend of resolution and hysteria, of barbarous vulgarity and boot-faced sobriety, which lies beneath the emotions of Ulster Protestantism. An evangelical religion which demanded that the Lambeg drum should be beaten 'until the knuckles of the drummers ran with blood' has clearly more than an economic motivation.

Such cultural history offers a timely antidote to those who have held that the sectarian conflict was always and only about jobs; but this book does not necessarily explode the Marxist claim that the current war is primarily economic in its underlying motivations. 1813 is not 1969, much less 1984. While Professor Lyons was right to suggest that the problem 'can only be understood in its historical context', he would have been wiser to add that the past decade provides many more telling insights into the roots of the current strife. As a contribution to cultural history, his book stops quite reasonably at 1939 with the outbreak of world war and the death of Yeats. But, as an attempt to explain the current conflict, this work is seriously marred by that terminal date. A great deal has happened in the intervening decades which Lyons could not discuss — the coming of the welfare state in the 1940s embraced with marked reluctance by the Unionists, the consequent emergence of articulate Catholic graduates in the 1960s, the failure of the Belfast régime to respond intelligently to their demands, and the ensuing violence of the 1970s. The overthrow of an upperclass Unionism (in the person of O'Neill), followed by the removal of mercantile Unionism (in the person of Faulkner), cleared the way for a proletarian leadership. The working-class leaders of militant Unionism in the 1980s bear scant resemblance to the

17 F.S.L. Lyons, *Culture and Anarchy in Ireland: 1890-1939* (Clarendon Press, Oxford, 1979), 144.

Carsons and Craigs of previous decades. Similarly, the contemporary IRA is filled with unemployed radicals and leftist revolutionaries, quite unlike the puritanical school-masters and idealistic civil servants satirised by Brendan Behan in the 1950s and 1960s. These changes are fundamentally economic in nature, just as the very emergence of the civil rights movement was chiefly made possible by the welfare state.

Professor Lyons, in his anxiety to prove that culture makes things happen, chose to end his book with a date which allowed him to neglect these salient points. If his thesis were explained to some of the current protagonists in the conflict, it would doubtless evoke bizarre responses. Is it really true that the difference between Glenn Barr and John Hume is attributable to a clash of cultures? How vital is the Gaelic tradition to a Dublin Government whose Minister for Education cannot even speak the Irish language? How deep is the loyalty of insurgent Unionism to the Anglo-Irish tradition? And to England, for that matter? 'For the Lenox-Conynghams of Ulster', remarked Lyons, 'service in the British Army was as inevitable as breathing'.[18] It was not quite so inevitable for many current Unionist leaders, whose 'loyalism' did not extend to enlisting in his majesty's forces to safeguard the world from the fascists. Mina Lenox-Conyngham's charming memoir of an ascendancy Big House is quoted by the author, who sees the following scene as quintessentially Anglo-Irish:

> ' . . . we like to remember the evening sunlight slanting through tall trees where jackdaws chatter, and making flickering patterns on walls hung with portraits, from which many a former occupant looks mysteriously down'.[19]

Whatever else this represents, it is certainly *not* what the UDA is fighting for.

The trouble with Lyons's exhilarating book is that its thesis works fairly well in its earlier nineteenth-century settings, but in modern Ulster men's emotions have been ruled not so much by culture as by cash. In a city of chronic unemployment such as Derry, money doesn't talk — it swears. In his zeal to prove that culture motivates political action, Lyons quoted those lines in which Yeats wondered if his play had sent out certain men the English shot. But poets are not the unacknowledged legislators of the world. As W.H. Auden observed with bitter resignation, such a description better fits the secret police. The

---

18   Ibid., 119.

19   Quoted ibid., 120.

denizens of Ballymurphy and the Shankill will hardly argue with that.

Conor Cruise O'Brien's *States of Ireland* confronts very squarely those decades of change which are unrecorded by F.S.L. Lyons and his stance, though polemical at the time of writing, has already become the orthodoxy in Dublin government circles. Yet his account of events contains scant reference to the economic factors which played such a part in the current phase of the struggle. The works of Lyons and O'Brien have been massively influential on British politicians of all parties and on British journalists of all papers, while books like Michael Farrell's *Northern Ireland: The Orange State* and Eamonn McCann's *War and an Irish Town* have not. The socialist analysts may be somewhat cavalier in their dismissal of culture as a potent source of distinctive symbols — symbols which reinforce and seem to legitimise the economic aspirations of the various Ulster factions. But it is at least arguable that they are a good deal nearer to the facts of the matter. An Irish reviewer of the texts spawned by the current crisis might wonder why they must turn exclusively to culture *or* to economics by way of explanation, when it is clear that the two go hand-in-hand, even if economics is leading the way. But he might also ask why the British intelligentsia choose to believe one set of explanations rather than the other. Is it because middle-class liberals are too cushioned by affluence to notice the way in which the world actually works? Is it that they fear to admit the reality of imperialist plunder which was the economic basis for that most admirable of systems, the welfare state? Is it that an audience of academics, journalists and politicians has a vested interest in the thesis that culture, and culture alone, makes things happen? Or could it be that Ireland is still deemed 'interesting and different', a place where the unexpected always happens, where men kill and die for abstract images and evocative symbols? This reading of the Irish as martyrs to abstraction — a reading sponsored most notoriously in the poetry of Yeats — is the greatest single obstacle to a full understanding of the situation in Ireland today. It bedevils attempts by students, both native and foreign, to understand the masterpieces of Irish literature; but it bedevils also the attempts by British well-wishers to understand John Bull's Other Island.

In the coming years British liberals must study Ulster Unionism and spell out to the English public the implications of its continuing support for such a régime. They must confront head-on the great paradox of modern Anglo-Irish relations — the fact that for fifty years one of the most civilised peoples in Europe maintained a one-party state on its own doorstep.

During those decades in which the English led the war on fascism and pioneered a welfare state, they continued to subsidise a régime characterised by religious bigotry and political repression. In the uncertain summer of 1936, the National Council for Civil Liberties complained in a report that Ulster Unionists had been allowed to create 'under the shadow of the British constitution a permanent machine of dictatorship'.[20] The report went on to compare Northern Ireland with the fascist régimes then current in Europe. In *Northern Ireland: The Orange State* Michael Farrell comments that 'in so far as the total identification of party and state was one of the hallmarks of European fascism, the comparison was apt'.[21] The British government paid no heed to the warnings of civil libertarians and the notorious Special Powers Act remained on the statute book. It became the envy of the uncivilised world. When Vorster introduced his Coercion Bill into the South African parliament in April 1963, he quelled all protest with the deathless observation that he 'would be willing to exchange all the legislation of that sort for one clause of the Northern Ireland Special Powers Act'.[22]

Unionist misrule has exacted a heavy cost not just in terms of British lives and money, but also in terms of its effect in eroding many of the best features of British democracy. As a result of its support for a decadent régime, Britain has been inculpated at Strasbourg. The reputation of the British Army has been damaged by its experience in Northern Ireland; and the American experience after Vietnam suggests that such poison may pass from the military into society at large. Ken Livingstone has wryly noted the fact that the police chief who presided over the conveyor-belts of Castlereagh now has responsibility for the London Metropolitan police. The 'laboratory-theory' is alive and well, and beginning to trouble the English left-wing. The supergrass system is now so patently unjust that even some of Ulster's hard-bitten judges have spoken of it with only half-concealed contempt. Moreover, the attempts by the English to root out corruption from their own body-politic have been hampered by their involvement in Ireland. When even the Tories could no longer stomach the racialism of

---

20 National Council for Civil Liberties, Report of a Commission of Inquiry appointed to examine the purposes and effect of the Civil Authorities (Special Powers) Acts, 1922 and 1933 (London, 1936). Reprinted London, 1972, p. 11 Quoted by Michael Farrell *Northern Ireland: The Orange State* (Pluto Press, London, 1976), 97.

21 Michael Farrell, *Northern Ireland: The Orange State*, 97.

22 'Quoted ibid., 93-4.

Enoch Powell, a ready berth was found for him in the heartlands of Ulster Unionism. The time may have come for the Tories to ponder the implications of their official designation as the 'Conservative and Unionist' Party. It is certainly time that British intellectuals applied themselves to a critical analysis of Unionism, what it represents, and what it is doing to Britain as a whole. They will be only too well aware that the collapse of French government in 1958 ocurred when the military became embroiled in a similar 'no-win' colonial situation.

British commentators are rightly outraged whenever London is bombed by the IRA, and they ask 'What kind of people could do such a thing?' But they never ask an equally pressing question — 'What kind of people are we supporting in Ulster?' The ignorance of Ireland among English people is considerable, but the ignorance of Ulster Unionism among English liberals is almost total. The current crisis has prompted most Irish people to re-examine some of their deepest historical assumptions, but it has as yet given rise to no similar self-questioning in England. On the contrary, a bomb in Harrod's gives all the hoariest anti-Irish clichés a new lease of life. If British writers are serious in their attempts to contribute to a solution, they must break out of the current impasse. To do that, they must cure themselves of their longstanding fixation on Irish nationalism and apply themselves to the study of Ulster Unionism. For most English liberals, this is a disagreeable prospect. The anonymous reviewer of Robert Kee's *The Green Flag* in the *Times Literary Supplement* of 26 May 1972 spoke for them all when he invoked

> . . . the superior attraction for the cultivated mind of the winding caravan of Irish nationalism with its poets, assassins, scholars, crackpots, parlour revolutionaries, windbags, mythopoeic essayists, traitors, orators from the scaffold, men of action, emerging from so long and so great suffering of the people to impart an almost mythic quality to their often futile and often brutal deeds — the superior attraction of that to the hard, assertive, obsessive, successful self-reliance of the Ulster Protestant which has about it as much imagination as is contained in a bowler hat.[23]

Because they are so sympathetic to the green flag, English

23 Quoted by Tom Nairn, *The Break-Up of Britain: Crisis and Neo-Nationalism* (New Left Books, London, 1977), 230. This book contains one of the few attempts by British Marxists to offer a sympathetic analysis of Ulster Unionism, but the author's information is obviously sparse and often inaccurate.

intellectuals have focussed on its tradition to the virtual exclusion of any informed assessment of the deeper meanings of Ulster Unionism. But, by their obsession with Irish nationalism, they have jeopardised its long-term prospects and the hopes of all Ireland and England for a solution. Since the time of Matthew Arnold, they have offered countless mythological analyses of the culture which England is nominally opposing. It is now time for them to conduct a pragmatic analysis of the Unionist culture which England is still actually supporting.

PRIMARY TEXTS

Brendan Behan, *The Hostage* (Methuen, London, 1958).

James Joyce, *Ulysses* (Harmondsworth, 1969).

Sean O'Casey, *The Plough and the Stars* in *Three Plays* (Macmillan, London, 1966).

George Bernard Shaw, *John Bull's Other Island* in *The Complete Plays of Bernard Shaw* (Odhams, London, 1937).

Oscar Wilde, *The Importance of Being Earnest* in *Plays* (Harmondsworth, 1954).

AFTERWORD

Denis Donoghue

Three of the six essays which constitute this book were published in 1983. I refer to Tom Paulin's *A New Look at the Language Question*, Seamus Heaney's *An Open Letter* and Seamus Deane's *Civilians and Barbarians*. On that occasion I reviewed the three in terms, I hope, responsive to the decorum of critical comment. When the other essays — by Declan Kiberd, Richard Kearney and again Seamus Deane — were published a year later, the question of my reviewing them did not arise; that is, no literary editor invited me to review them. On the present occasion, considerations of decorum suggest a different tone. I am not now reviewing some parts of the work but commenting upon it in a larger setting. What the difference is, I am not sure I could explain. But in any case it would be improper of me to ignore the fact that I have discussed some of these essays and commented on them. To meet this consideration I propose to reprint the review, adding two minor qualifications by way of footnotes, and then to go further in the direction indicated by the several essays in hand.

Field Day is a company established a few years ago in Derry, the spiritual home of its directors Brian Friel, Seamus Heaney, Seamus Deane, Tom Paulin, Stephen Rea and David Hammond: respectively a playwright, three poets, an actor and, I gather, a walking saint.[1] Friel's plays gave the group its first ventures, Heaney's poems indicated that something more formal than the several individual efforts might be attempted. Field Day has now published three pamphlets, presumably to give the group a discursive and argumentative capacity.

Tom Paulin's essay is based on his understanding that the question of language 'is a question about nationhood and government'. He is concerned with the implications, for both

---

[1] This reference to David Hammond is too cryptic. He is, in daily life, a singer and a broadcaster.

nationhood and government, of the situation of spoken and written language in Ireland. He doesn't mention, but indeed well knows, that the British Government's policy has been to acknowledge that regional accents and dictions exist, but that it is not necessary to take much account of the whole range of dialects. The development of local radio and television may make a difference, but for the time being the privileged position of Standard English is to be maintained. In effect, Standard English is the speech of educated people in London and the South.

The clearest defence of this policy I have heard recently came from Robert Burchfield, editor of the Supplementary Volumes of the *OED*. In a television conversation with Bernard Levin, he said that while indeed millions of people in Britain speak various dialects, Standard English still embodies their aspirations. He meant that if these people want to qualify themselves for a good job in London, they must learn and speak Standard English. Burchfield has now established at Oxford a service by which anyone, by a telephone call, can learn what the correct Standard English usage in a particular case is.

The political consequence of Standard English is clear: it testifies to the unity of Great Britain at a level superior to any tremors of regional loyalty to be found in Scotland, Wales or elsewhere.

Paulin gives an interesting account, necessarily brief, of the development of English dictionaries. Standard English is defined and embodied in the *OED*. Webster's *Dictionary of American English* was a nationalist gesture offered by a linguist who thought of America as a young and vivid country with a correspondingly lively language at a time — the year was 1780 — when the language of Britain was already corrupt. Nationalism in language has persisted in the USA from Webster to H. L. Mencken, William Carlos Williams, Charles Olson and, by now, virtually every American writer.

It is not clear what this history has to do with the Irish question. There is no Dictionary of Irish English, though there are dictionaries of the English of Scotland, Canada, and Jamaica. As a result, there are lots of homeless words, spoken in our houses and fields but not acknowledged in any official way. Some of them turn up in Heaney's poems, in Patrick Kavanagh's, and in work of other poets and novelists, but they are not generally understood. A dictionary, Paulin argues, would give them stability and resonance. True: but

Webster doesn't offer a model. His *Dictionary* is just as devoted to Standard American as the *OED* is to Standard English.

Paulin seems to favour a federal dictionary of Irish English in which the regional words would be fully recognised:

> Thus in Ireland there would exist three fully-fledged languages — Irish, Ulster Scots, and Irish English. Irish and Ulster Scots would be preserved and nourished, while Irish English would be a form of modern English which draws on Irish, the Yola and Fingallian dialects, Ulster Scots, Elizabethan English. Hiberno-English, and American English.

As for Irish writers: they can't be content with Standard English, according to Paulin, since its only home is Westminster. It might be possible for Irish poets and novelists to resort to the kind of 'cosmopolitan English' of which Paulin's only produced example is Samuel Beckett's style: a curious suggestion, unless Paulin means to impose on his colleagues the quaint procedure of writing in English while living in Paris. He thinks that such a cosmopolitan English might make available to creative writers 'a pure civility which should not be pressed into the service of history or politics'.

What the discursive writers are to do, Paulin doesn't say; but he is notably severe on the diverse styles of F. S. L. Lyons. Owen Dudley Edwards, Benedict Kiely, and some unnamed writers who 'appear to have been infected by Frank Delaney's saccharine gabbiness'.

Seamus Heaney's essay is a verse letter to Blake Morrison and Andrew Motion, editors of *The Penguin Book of Contemporary British Poetry* (1982). The letter is prefaced by a quotation from Gaston Bachelard:

> What is the source of our first suffering?
> It lies in the fact that we hesitated to speak . . .
> It was born in the moment when we accumulated silent things within us.

The silent thing Heaney has accumulated within him, apparently, is a touch of resentment or dismay that he finds himself called a British poet. I think Bachelard had something more sublime or more aboriginal in view. Besides, Heaney's protest came slowly. It takes a long time to gather the poems for an anthology: a year or two, not less. Heaney could have withdrawn his work from the hands of Morrison and Motion, even if he had been coaxed into giving it in the first place. Still, I suppose the point shouldn't be made with any severity. Feelings are not punctual things; dismay and resentment come when they are ready and not before.

The letter itself is charming. Heaney is too nice to be a satirist. His political satires seem to me fully-throated but half-hearted, as if he disliked the tone the occasions forced upon him; as well he might. He is best, warmest, and most telling in meditative and descriptive lyrics. The new poem answers its occasion without transcending it. Reading it, I kept wondering what Austin Clarke, in his last years, would have made of a similar predicament. Many of Clarke's satires arose from irritations no graver than Heaney's, but Clarke's talent was never happier than while vexing its objects. He did not allow himself to be inhibited by charm. Heaney's smile gets in the way when he tries to write rough stuff.

But it would be foolish to underrate Heaney's rhetorical skill. Smile he may. A lesser poet, rejecting 'British' and insisting on 'Irish', might be tempted to paint the green more ardently than ever. Heaney tells his editorial friends that his passport is green, but he takes care to show them that no disability is entailed. The poem alludes with supreme rhetorical ease to T. S. Eliot, Yeats, Milton, Synge, Michel Foucault, Donald Davie, Philip Larkin, and a book by Miroslav Holub translated by Stuart Frieberg and Dana Habova and published in Ohio. There are casual references to English, indeed to British magazines, abbreviated as the *TLS* and *LRB*. Even to TV jargon; Kojak's 'no way', someone's 'not my thing'. Eliot's 'Tereu Tereu' becomes 'tooraloo' and runs out to play with 'royal blue'.

I'm not sure what Morrison and Motion, lacking Paulin's desired dictionary, will make of the mock-rueful stanza:

> For weeks and months I've messed about,
> Unclear, embarrassed and in doubt,
> Footered, havered, spraughled, wrought
> Like Shauneen Keogh,
> Wondering should I write it out
> Or let it go.

— especially since recourse to *The Playboy of the Western World* will not discover Shaun Keogh speaking any of the hard words. No matter. Morrison and Motion are canny enough to divine what Heaney is saying: I'm Irish indeed, but don't think I can't handle myself on the international circuit or negotiate the several traditions any good contemporary British poet assumes he can command.

There is one respect in which the poem, without floating free of its occasion, annotates it winningly: in a meditative brooding on the question of names and naming:

> Right names were the first foundation
> For telling truth

Heaney truly says. An earlier stanza plays upon the provenance of a proper name:

> You'll understand I draw the line
> At being robbed of what is mine,
> My *patria*, my deep design
>   To be at home
> In my own place and dwell within
>   Its proper name.

The sentiment is well established, as it happens, in both English and Irish poetry, though *patria* grounds it, for the time being, on a Latin — Virgil, Horace — richer than either English or Irish in this particular feeling. The poem ends with an elaborate allusion to an episode in Holub's *Saggital Section* in which another man from a society regularly disdained insists upon having his proper name and rejects the official substitute.

Now for real anger: Seamus Deane's. His theme is ostensibly academic, the power of an official discourse to impose judgments and penalties without having to state a case in court or call witnesses. I infer that Deane has been reading Foucault, and especially his attacks on ideological systems — of prisons, the treatment of the insane, the definition of sexuality — which coerce the individual without even telling him that he is to be constrained. Ideology in that sense is a force of society which pretends to be a force of nature and therefore doesn't need to be justified. Deane's particular concern is with the tradition in which English authorities purveyed a stereotype of the Irish character: to be Irish meant to be barbarous, drunken, lazy, and generally dissolute. Illiterate clowns, every Pat of them.

Deane quotes several English writers, from Spenser in 1596 to Coleridge in 1814, and all to the same rhetorical effect. The case is axiomatic: the Irish were never properly subdued, English common law did not displace old loyalties based on kinship of clan, the sense of law was always regarded in Ireland as secondary to the sense of conscience. Being Catholics and therefore turned toward Rome, the Irish accepted the word of their priests rather than the letter of a secular law. Father Mathew's crusade for temperance was based upon Catholic teaching and the rights of an informed conscience outraged by gluttony; not upon the fact that drunken conduct was illegal or criminal.

Deane's survey of these matters is far too brisk, they require more detailed analysis than he has space for. He is anxious to show that, according to this English typology, the Irish have been regarded as lawless by definition. The demonology includes not only drunken Paddy but the criminal and now bomb-throwing Teigue.

At this point in the argument I found myself wanting more evidence, not just a swift survey of English moral and literary history without a succinct typology of the coerced Irish at the end of it.

Deane identifies the bomb-throwing IRA as 'the Irish'; a strange epitome, since the vast majority of 'the Irish' refuse to let the IRA speak or act in their name.[2] He says that the British Army in the North, 'who wear uniforms, and live in barracks, and drive armoured cars, operate checkpoints etc. etc., kill with impunity because they represent, they embody Law'.

There is a daunting amount of evidence for this view; but in every country the representatives of the law are privileged against the criminal. If a policeman in New York shoots a man, everybody assumes, at least to begin with, that he had cause. It may emerge that he hadn't, but the presupposition is that he had. Besides, 'kill with impunity' is a sweeping summary of recent legal history in the North; though I'd like to be more certain than I am that a soldier who shoots to kill will be punished.

Deane's anger is most insistent on two matters. He is angry with the Churches for using the concept of an immutable 'Natural Law' or 'Moral Code' — the irony of the capitals is Deane's — more directly against the terrorist than against the soldier:

> There is an interesting political distinction between the appeals made by clergy to terrorists and those made to the forces of Law and Order. The first are made to individuals, loners, to come in out of the moral cold, to cease disgracing the cause they ostensibly represent; the second are made to a corporate body, not to the individual.

But priests see themselves as trying to save an individual's soul, a more urgent matter, from that standpoint, than trying to improve the behaviour of the British Army. To be fair, they often protest against the behaviour of the Army, as Cardinal O'Fiaich did recently. But it is true that priests, like most people, want to see the bloodshed in the North come to an end. Like other people, they prefer a quiet life to destruction and death. Does Deane really want them to urge the bomb-throwers on to grander deeds of murder and suicide?

---

2   On second thoughts, I don't think there is enough evidence in Deane's essays to justify this sentence.

The second source of Deane's anger is the fact — and I think he is right in this — that political and moral discourse has distorted the situation that provoked it:

> Nothing demonstrated this more than the Peace Movement, one of the most successful of all political exploitations of a moral code which was in fact a political code. Hardly anyone remembers that the incident which sparked the movement off began with the killing of an IRA man, who was driving a car, by a British soldier — who was himself in no danger. The charismatic movement in Catholicism and the evangelical movement in Protestantism combined to display, in front of the cameras, the longing for peace by a population disturbed by the guerrillas within their ranks — not by the army, or the police, or the unemployment, housing conditions and so forth.

A distortion, indeed. I never had much confidence in the Peace Movement. But it was an attempt, however naively made, to shout *Stop*, and to set aside the laying of blame.

I assume that the three essays were written independently: their styles and tones make that fairly clear. But they have one feature in common, a rejection of the authority exercised from the centre. Paulin speaks up for the recognition of several dialects, unsubmissive to Standard English. Heaney rejects the tone of the centre, the imperative word from London. Deane denounces what he regards as an ideological conspiracy of Church and State to conceal from people the truth of their desires and aspirations.

I'm more troubled by Deane, on this occasion, than by Paulin or Heaney; more worried that he may be, in some appalling respects, right, and that his being right won't help the situation we care about.

Let us assume that most people in the North regard themselves as either Unionists or Nationalists. Unionists want to remain within the United Kingdom; they accept the British royal family and the Parliament at Westminster as their symbols of loyalty and authority. Nationalists repudiate these symbols and look rather to Ireland, the island as a whole, and to Dublin as its centre. Let us assume, too, that most of the people who think of themselves as Unionists or Nationalists have inherited their sentiments and haven't interrogated them: besides, what they mainly want is a peaceful, prosperous life. They have never drawn blood, or even thought of doing such a thing.

But there are some Unionists and some Nationalists who are not willing to rest upon vague sentiments. Suppose they were invited to express themselves. The Unionists would say something along these lines. 'My family has lived in the North of Ireland since 1615. Between 1609 and 1630, it is estimated,

14,500 British men, many with their families, migrated from East Anglia, the West Midlands, Chester and other places, to the North. We did not immediately displace the Gaelic Irish; though gradually we secured possession of the better land, and the natives moved to poorer land and higher ground. We farmed, and set up small communities which extended themselves to county towns. When Britain developed new industries, we took part in the development: linen, especially. We gained many of the advantages of the Industrial Revolution. Belfast became a city like Manchester and Glasgow, not like Ascendancy Dublin. We remained Protestants, Presbyterians mostly, and thought of Catholics as good enough people provided they stayed in their patch and minded their own business. We wanted to be good neighbours but not friends. We were happy when we got our own state, Northern Ireland, and our own little Parliament at Stormont, and even if we ran things as a one-party government, that was our right. If the Catholics don't like it here, they can go South, where there is a Rome-ridden state they may or may not enjoy. We intend to hold what we have: and we will be extremely vigilant, watching for the first sign that a British Government is thinking of taking away our rights. Ian Paisley is our man.'

The Nationalist would reply: 'My family has been in Ireland for centuries before 1615. Whatever scholars tell us about the high kings of Ireland, we hold that in historically modern times Ireland is one country, a small island, with a distinctive culture, a language destroyed by the British and — I must concede — by some of our own people who saw, in the nineteenth century, that English was the language of education and advancement. We are mainly a Catholic people. We regard as a monstrosity the Anglo-Irish Treaty that set up Northern Ireland. Unionists were never entitled to six counties, even when they insisted on separating themselves from the rest of the country. Perhaps three and a fraction of a fourth would have been fair, but Unionists conspired with the British Government to take six, on the device of gerrymandered constituencies which effectively ensured a one-party government, "a Protestant Parliament for a Protestant people". For sixty years this monstrosity has persisted, sustained by Westminster, ignored by Dublin. In the South the Fianna Fáil Party, ostensibly Republican, goes through the annual motion, at the Ard dFéis, of repeating their call for Irish unity: for the rest of the year, the matter is quietly set aside. The Fine Gael Party — now with a few Labour members the Coalition Government — has never felt strongly about Partition. Their fathers accepted it in the first place. Garret Fitzgerald, like his former colleague Conor Cruise

O'Brien, is engaged in the exercise of making Partition a permanent and acceptable feature of life on this island, in return for a few American dollars. We have lost whatever confidence we ever had in the half-hearted SDLP. So our only hope is in Sinn Fein and the Provisional IRA. Killing is not what we want, but the British have never paid attention to Ireland until dead soldiers, dead policemen and dead aristocrats have concentrated their minds.'

We may take such sentiments as providing a context for the present book. I don't claim that the two speeches adequately testify to the range of sentiments in the case.

Since 1968, when the latest phase of the Troubles — as they have long been called — began in the North, there have been many attempts to explain the situation and to resolve it. Most of these have assumed that the situation is a problem for which, it follows, a solution must be found. No one has been willing to think that it may be a condition, a state of affairs, rather than a problem, and that there may be no answer to it, no solution except to put up with it. Is there a solution to the 'problem' of the Middle East?

About ten years ago a number of teachers at University College, Dublin, started thinking of the North in philosophic terms. Sensitive to the fact that most situations in Ireland have been examined in a narrow and local context, they proposed to extend the setting and to bring to bear upon Ireland and especially upon the North the considerations currently available in European philosophy. They established *The Crane Bag* as a forum for these debates, a magazine in which it became a standard experience to find Irish culture examined by reference to Wittgenstein and Derrida.

Richard Kearney has been a leading force in these discussions. As a philosopher, he has carried political issues to a high level of abstraction. His mind has appeased itself by recourse to large dichotomies — the sacred and the profane, *mythos* and *logos*, piety and secularism, Mother Ireland and Molly Bloom, Celtic Paganism and Irish Catholicism. 'What is required', he says in the essay in this book, 'is a radical interrogation of those mythic sedimentations from our *past* and those mythic aspirations for our *future* which challenge our *present* sense of ourselves, which disclose other possibilities of being'. We must never cease, he says, 'to keep our mythological images in dialogue with history'. What this seems to mean is that Kearney wants the best of both vocabularies: the reverberation and radiance of *mythos,* the critical intelligence of *logos.*

But there is, indeed, a problem. Kearney starts his essay by setting 'a *logos* of rational critique' in a stringent relation to 'a *mythos* of irrational mystification'. He ends by saying, in effect, that we need both, and the values they propose. In a certain mood he would deconstruct our myths by appeal to *logos*. But there is no producible reason why the deconstructive act should end at that point. What makes *logos* immune to a further critique? A dialogue with history? But history is not solid ground. No word in contemporary thought has been more effectively undermined than history: it is hard to use the word at all without seeing it dissolve into fiction or fancy. This is the trouble with a sustained critique: there is no end to it, nothing is immune. While Kearney wants to have the best of *mythos* and *logos,* a severe Derridean is already preparing to subvert both in endless linguistic play.

These are heart-mysteries as well as problems. It is true that Yeats hoped to found a new sense of being Irish upon ancient symbols, holy places, legends and lore, upon 'a memory beyond all individual memories', in a phrase Kearney quotes. It is also true that Yeats was susceptible to his visions, and liable to become enchanted by his dreams. But he also knew that 'history is necessity until it takes fire in someone's head and becomes freedom or virtue', as he wrote in his Diary of 1930. What did he mean? Or rather: is it still history when it has become freedom or virtue? It would be wrong to assume that Yeats's thinking on myth, symbol and history was simple, or that he was enslaved to his idiom.

But I am not surprised that some of the writers in this book are irritated and frustrated by the grandeurs they have inherited. Two years ago, this sentiment was expressed in a series of televised lectures under the title *Ireland: Dependence and Independence,* a collaboration between Radio Telefís Eireann and University College, Dublin; a sour affair in which the lecturers showed that they were mainly disgruntled and not at all exhilarated by the possession of a notable literature and, at the least, a suggestive history. Kearney, Deane and Kiberd were among the lecturers on that occasion, but it was Kiberd who most clearly, and most sourly, expressed the pervasive mood.

If you were persuaded by Kiberd, you would regard the Easter Rising as a misfortune; or at least as a movement most unfortunately led. If it had been directed by James Connolly rather than by Padraig Pearse, then it would have been a socialist act, part of a larger movement, international socialism. It would not have been defined in Gaelic and Catholic terms, and suffused by the vocabulary of blood-sacrifice and martyr-dom. Pearse could not have taken upon himself the role of Christ. He may have called Cuchulainn to his side in the Post Office, if Yeats's poem 'The Statues' is right; but more effect-ively for the rhetoric of the Rising, he called Christ to his side.

Indeed, while several of the writers in this book brood upon conflicts between Yeats and Pearse, they also see them together, and they think of them as leading modern Ireland astray; Pearse, toward the glory of sacrifice and martyrdom, in which the most extreme defeat is transformed to the sweetest victory, and death becomes the most glorious form of life; Yeats, toward an infatuated sense of the fate of being Irish. 'We Irish, born into that ancient sect . . . '.

This is Deane's theme, in part, and Heaney's too. Deane's consideration of Yeats and Joyce sets them as far apart as ever, but in an unusual way. Reading Yeats, we are to think of style as the expression of communal history governed by a single and singular imagination. Yeats's individual style then becomes 'the signature of the community's deepest self'. Reading the later Joyce, we reflect upon 'the atomisation of community . . . in a multitude of equivalent, competing styles'. Deane doesn't explain why the styles in Joyce are necessarily in competition or, if they are, where precisely the competition is joined. They seem to me to exist as if in separate chapters of *Ulysses*; or to achieve a strangely moving accommodation in the waters of *Finnegans Wake*. But no matter: what troubles Deane, to begin with, is the idea of a destiny awaiting each of the communities in the North. Each destiny is announced with a corresponding style which insists that it is the true name and delivers the very essence of that community. In the earlier essay Deane spoke of this motif as one of obligatory role-playing, but I assume he has found that metaphor not entirely helpful. He still holds to the idea that to be a Catholic or a Protestant in the North is to have one's life already inscribed, understood by minds preceding one's own.

Yeats again takes much of the blame. According to Deane, Yeats has transmitted to us the rhetoric of Romantic Ireland, and therefore the quest, as our true task, for the essence of our lives as Irish men and women. Deane denounces our readiness to accept 'the mystique of Irishness as an inalienable feature of our writing and, indeed, of much else in our culture'. He alludes to Yeats, Daniel O'Connell, Parnell, De Valera and Synge — each of them determined to project his own imagin-ation upon the Irish people. It is sometimes taken as a sign of De Valera's spiritual vanity that he proposed to divine what the people of Ireland wanted by looking into his own heart. I have never understood the rebuke: where else should he have looked? What does any leader do, if not project his image of himself upon the people he leads? Deane evidently does not believe 'in the incarnation of the nation in the individual'. He is free to believe or not; but hardly to imply that the nation — if such an entity exists — is incarnated in anything else. Perhaps I have misunderstood him.

It is a tribute to Yeats that Deane finds him largely responsible for our obsession with the fate of being Irish. But he well knows that Yeats didn't invent the interest; Renan, Matthew Arnold and many other writers anticipated him in seeking the Celtic element or the Celtic spirit. Deane also knows that the interest persists and is found in writers who can't be regarded as Yeats's slaves. What else is Heaney's *Open Letter* but a complaint that his identity — it is his word — has been rudely forced; and it follows that he has an interest in expounding the identity. If Deane were to argue that it is time we gave up concerning ourselves with the search for an 'essence' which we take as the spiritual mark of nationhood — of being Irish — the argument would be reasonable. But an ironist would then remark that thousands of people in Ireland today show no interest in discovering such an interest, and every interest in making a lot of money. So where are we?

But in any case Deane doesn't pursue the logic of such an argument. 'It is about time we put aside the idea of essence', he says, ' — that hungry Hegelian ghost looking for a stereotype to live in'. But 'stereotype' abuses the issue. Hegel would not have been content to call his *geist* a stereotype. Besides, why is it so dreadful for Irishmen to try to understand themselves, and to embody their understanding in an image or a narrative? Aren't Jews constantly engaged with the destiny of being Jews? Aren't Americans? Surely Deane knows that President Reagan's dealings with El Salvador and Nicaragua are not merely essays in foreign policy but acts of piety toward his sense of what it means to be an American, President of the Redeemer Nation?

Deane says that a new anthology of Irish writing of the past few centuries would show that 'the myth of Irishness, the notion of Irish unreality, the notions surrounding Irish eloquence' are in fact 'political themes upon which the literature has battened to an extreme degree since the nineteenth century when the idea of national character was invented'. My own view is that people were concerned with their national characters before Christ was crucified. But I agree that the question became virtually a fixation in the nineteenth century. Nevertheless, even if a new anthology were to disclose what Deane expects it to disclose, the fact that these motifs turn out to be political themes wouldn't solve anything. Like his colleagues in this book, Deane is determined to think that you have solved a problem when you have translated it from metaphysics into politics. There is no reason to believe you have: you may have merely created a new problem.

I was surprised, reading Deane, that he did not suggest that the answer to Yeats is Joyce: instead of Romantic Ireland, let us go international, or at least European. But he doesn't suggest that recourse. Indeed, he evidently doesn't share the infatuation with *Finnegans Wake* which we find in many French critics who celebrate the book as if it constituted the final defeat of bourgeois liberalism. At the end of *Heroic Styles* he seems to say merely: a plague on all your houses. We have created 'an idea of Ireland as provincialism incarnate', and to escape from it we have become 'virtuoso metropolitans'. These are worn oppositions, he says. But I am not sure who has worn them, or represented the choice in those terms. His final sentence asks us to start again, re-write and re-read our texts. That, he says, 'will enable new writing, new politics, unblemished by Irishness, but securely Irish'.

I wonder. A man is not on oath in his last sentences, but I can't see that Deane is saying anything more than: you'll be a better Irishman if you don't think about what it means to be one. That may be true. But I don't see why such a vow of self-denial should be imposed upon Irishmen alone. Indeed, Deane regularly underestimates the force of nationalism. As a sentiment, nationalism has for so long been despised that its continued vigour is astonishing. Indeed, it thrives best in the institutions designed to transcend it. When Ireland joined the EEC we mainly had in view that the financial advantage to us would be immense. Those who wanted to evade such a sordid consideration maintained that the EEC would enable its members to transcend the shoddy imperatives of nationalism. Not so: every issue in the EEC is pursued along strictly national-istic lines — Irish milk, Irish fishing-rights, French wine, Britain's financial contribution, and so forth. Indeed, it is chimerical to think that Ireland will try to understand itself by not thinking of itself as a small island, a nation-state, with a certain history which still appears to have consequences.

The interest of the present book is to be found, I suggest, among these concerns. If the Troubles had not flared up again in 1968, these writers would not now, I think, be reading Yeats, Joyce, O'Casey, Shaw and the other Irish writers in a spirit of anger and resentment. They would have been willing, as I was, to take our poetic masters pretty much on their own terms and as they came. I have always assumed that myths are devised as explanatory narratives alternative to circumstance and contingency, and I have read the Anglo-Irish writers in that way: myths have never been transcriptions of quotidian events. I can't report that I find the present form of interrogation entirely persuasive. I am reminded of a passage in Hans Blumenberg's *The Legitimacy of the Modern Age,* which speaks of 'giving oneself the history that sets one free of history'. The desire is easy to understand: it is clearly appeased by myth-making. But also by the attempt, as in this book, to get rid of the myths we have inherited. In that scale of things we are all about equal.

The man to beat is Yeats. I can readily understand that his sense of Ireland, his high style, his equestrian rhetoric, amount to a challenge so oppressive that a self-respecting writer is impelled to reject it. But while an argument can be refuted, and a thesis undermined, a vision can only be answered by another one. I don't think any historian's evidence would make a difference to Yeats's vision, or dislodge it from our minds. Only another vision, as complete as Yeats's, could take its place. Where could one look for such a thing? Not, I'm sure, from a poet writing in Irish, immune to the Yeatsian clamour, his mind filled with quite different idioms and reverberations from sources Yeats never knew.

Meanwhile, we argue. I assume the aim of the Field Day writers is to clear the ground. Their work is important, I believe, not because of the latitude of the ground yet cleared, but because they have made it impossible for us to rest content and unquestioning in the presence of Yeatsian charms. We have long known that Yeats has had a design for us, we have felt his solicitation; but we have not been vigilant, as the Field Day writers have been, or recognised the degree to which Yeats's rhetoric has taken possession of our affections.